"An inspirational must read! I am truly inspired as every person will be. These compelling stories need to be told and shared with all. I recommend this book to every man, woman and child in the land."

- **Joey Jackson, Criminal Defense Attorney and CNN Legal Analyst**

"WOW! I am truly inspired by these AMAZING stories! This book is a must read for every age group and then shared to every age group. What a Great message to give to the world. True Champions!"

- **Derek L. Anderson Sr., NBA Champion and Philanthropist**

"Inspiring! This book is more than a collection of stories, it's a tool every person should have in their hand. It is a treasury of experiences sang to the world in the key of 'male.' The stories are insightful, gripping, and worth hearing. I recommend this book without reservation!"

- **Terrell Fletcher, Former NFL Player, current Pastor of The City of Hope International Church**

THE

C.A.L.L.

**INSPIRING STORIES FOR YOUNG MEN ABOUT
CHARACTER, ACCOUNTABILITY, LOVE, AND LEADERSHIP**

COACHDIVERSITY
—— PRESS ——

The C.A.L.L.: Inspiring Stories For Young Men About Character, Accountability, Love, and Leadership

ISBN-13: 978-1536896572
ISBN-10: 1536896578

Published by:
CoachDiversity Press
5501 Merchants View Square #760
Haymarket, VA 20169
www.coachdiversitypress.com

www.7-publishing.com
Editors: Sherman Turntine, Jennifer Wilkes, and Maleeka Hollaway
Cover Design by Angela Wesley

Contents

Introduction

By Dr. Towanna Freeman

"The greatest glory in living lies not in never falling, but in rising every time we fall." - Nelson Mandela

My spirit was stirred on the evening of February 26, 2012, as I was watching the 11 o'clock news describe the unfolding events that led to the death of Trayvon Martin, a young Black man with a life of promise ahead of him.

And that evening, as the mother of a son, I took Trayvon's death personally as I watched that news broadcast. It was my wake-up call.

Since then, the lives of many more young men like Trayvon have been senselessly brought to a premature end. That particular news broadcast reawakened my desire to positively pour directly into the lives of young men – offering them a different reality and giving them new hope.

So I asked myself, *what could I do to contribute to the mission to uplift, inspire and guide young black men and break the cycle of violence in the black community?* Particularly in a 21st century America where the Black Lives Matter movement is calling for a united focus on issues of race, class, gender, nationality, sexuality, disability, and state-sponsored violence – what could **I** do?

As a successful business woman and social entrepreneur, mentors have played important roles in my life at all stages from when I was in middle school and even now, as an adult. This is the reason why I founded the Young Women's Empowerment Network in 1999, a nonprofit organization dedicated to providing role models, emotional, and social help and the necessary resources helping teen girls (ages 14-18) realize their potential to succeed in life. Thousands of young women throughout the U.S. have participated in my leadership training workshops and conferences. I am passionate about empowering our youth.

It was in 2003 that I decided to form a partnership with District of Columbia Public Schools and I expanded my community outreach to include young men (ages 14-18). Together we created a series of empowerment conferences titled, The C.A.L.L. For Young Men.

I saw, felt, and witnessed the difference that The C.A.L.L. events made. I saw, felt and witnessed how young men like you were touched and inspired. A ripple effect of change and transformation was unfolding before my eyes. That's when the acronym "C.A.L.L." was initially born, with these four letters representing Character, Accountability, Love and Leadership.

Character is built over time through your actions or your patterns of behavior as it relates to self-respect, keeping your word to yourself and to others, and making choices based on what is right rather than what is easy.

Accountability is your willingness to take ownership for your choices, the consequences arising from them, and for your own happiness. It is the opposite of blaming, complaining, procrastinating, and finger-pointing.

Love is a strong and powerful emotion that can be a positive force in your life. It is my hope that you learn to define what love means to you and all the different ways you can show love throughout your lifetime.

Leadership is the ability to inspire or influence others toward the achievement of a goal or the fulfillment of an intention. Leadership is about setting direction in your life, having a vision for yourself, being able to map out where you want to go in life, and being able to get there. When you bring others along with you – even better.

You may have received this book as a gift from someone who cares about you and your future, or maybe this was a book you chose for a reading assignment. No matter how you were introduced to *The C.A.L.L.,* it was placed in your life because you matter. You make a difference.

This book is a collection of stories written by black men, ages 19-68, who are mentors, fathers, motivational speakers, business professionals, coaches and community leaders. They have shared their inspiring personal stories on how they faced and overcame, odds such as growing up in fatherless homes; becoming the first in their families to graduate from college; surviving gang violence, and overcoming homelessness.

The C.A.L.L. is my response to the community's dire need to uplift, inspire and guide young men like you by providing a resource written by black men for young black men.

It is my hope that this book reaches young men across the country and activates new ways of thinking, new levels of self-confidence, and a deeper understanding of how to build character and integrity. I also hope that you learn the power of being accountable; how to love yourself and forgive others; how to achieve your goals, and lead in your own life.

You matter.

You are here to make a difference.

Life's challenges are meant to mold you, refine you, and develop a strong sense of resilience within you.

There is an entire community of people who care about you and your success.

On behalf of me and all of the co-authors that lovingly and transparently shared their stories within these pages, it is our hope that this book touches your heart, encourages you to keep going, motivates you to push forward, and helps you to create new possibilities for your life.

You are invited to answer the call!

Dr. Towanna Freeman

. . . .

1

Dead Last
By Alonzo M. Kelly

"Dead Last is better than Did Not Finish, and definitely better than Never Started." - Anonymous

I was born in Detroit, Michigan, in the 70s, and I had no choice in the matter. I was born into a situation where my mother could not take care of me at the time. I spent the first 10 years of my life in nine different foster homes. On top of attending a school where I was one of the few black kids, I didn't know who my father was – so that support was nonexistent. The circumstances of my situation had me feeling like I was constantly finishing dead last. If life was a race to the finish line, I felt as though everyone, and I do mean everyone, was finishing ahead of me.

When I was about 11, my grandmother was given custody of me. She sent me to a boarding school seven hours away, and I never lived at home again. It was difficult at first because I had convinced myself that I was only at that school because I was being pushed away. Adjusting to my new life in a boarding school was like getting excited about the peas on your plate. No kid wants to eat peas, but then one day you just realize that they're good for you.

It was still challenging. There are very few boarding schools that are all young black kids. I was sent from Detroit to a boarding school in Wisconsin. One day, I'm hanging out in the streets of Detroit and the next morning I'm staring at my first tractor and cow. Of all the adjustments I've had to make in my life, this was a situation I was not accustomed to.

If life was a race, everything around me made me feel like I was coming in last place. When it came to my family, I felt like I was in last place. My grandmother only had two children. My cousins had a bond that was special among themselves and my mother had a daughter who was 10 years younger than me. There were no fathers involved in any of our lives and no uncles to rely on as male figures to help guide me in my journey.

When it came to grades, I felt like I was in last place. I was bussed to an elementary school where I had to learn the language in a Polish community that was not yet ready to embrace diversity in the classroom. When it came to socioeconomics, I definitely felt like I was in last place. This is not too difficult to understand when your grandmother is a cashier at a grocery store and was financially responsible for not only her adult children, but also her grandchildren.

Something finally clicked for me when I was a teenager. I started to notice something about the world around me. It became clear that I was coming in dead last in the same community where the very same people who were teasing me had quit. They stopped going to school. Indifference had set in so much so that their future stopped mattering to them. Despite the noise, from all of their teasing, I was still attempting to move forward instead of quitting. I put them in that category of "Did Not Finish."

I also noticed another group of people when I was younger, again, who always had something to say, always had some negative opinion about what was going on in my life. Of course the reality about this group set in as well. It is far easier to judge and ridicule that which you have not given yourself permission to attempt. While I continued on my journey, admittedly stumbling along the way, these same folks never attempted to do anything to get themselves out of their current circumstance.

Whatever I attempted or was attempting to do with my life at that time, the "Did Not Finishers" were making me feel like I was coming in last place. But actually, they were commenting from the sidelines of my life. It's like the person at a professional sporting event yelling from the stands, "You suck," but has never even tried out for a "team" and has never set foot on a sports field.

The Only One

Being one of the 15 to 20 guys on my block, I woke up one day and realized that I was the *only* one that graduated from high school and was on pace to graduate from college. I went on to be the only one that actually did graduate from college. I started to feel pretty good about that "Last Place" feeling that for years had plagued my thoughts and soul. Never before had I been so excited to have experienced "Dead Last" until I noticed what happened to people that "Did Not Finish" and those that "Never Started."

There are all kinds of reasons and opportunities out there that are designed, both intentionally and unintentionally, for us not to succeed. Most of us are not born into a situation where mom is a doctor and father is a lawyer, so the wind may seem like it's in your face. If through no fault of your own, you are born into a situation that seems like it would be impossible to escape, remember a simple truth about headwinds: planes and kites take off against the wind. Every challenge we give ourselves permission to attack head-on, can result in life lessons and learning experiences that allow us to soar higher in life. This invaluable lesson is not taught in classrooms. What you will gain by not giving up will forever give you an advantage when dealing with the challenges in society, particularly for us as black men. It's time we embrace the headwind.

"I Can't Help That"

I finally learned who my father was when I was 33 years old. Throughout my high school and college years, I had no idea who he was. I know my grandmother did her best to teach me how to be a man. However, I think a man's presence and guidance is needed to teach me how to be a man. The person that I was most comfortable with teaching me the lessons of manhood was a priest. We did not share all the same experiences, but I did look to him for direction and for help in managing conflict and better communication with others.

It was difficult to understand at first, but my grandmother had this phrase that she would always say, no matter what the situation. Her phrase was, "I can't help that." For every reason I would give her why something could not or should not be done, she would come back with, "I can't help that." "Grandmother, I can't do my homework because my book is old." "I can't help that." "Grandmother, I can't get to practice because it's too far away and you don't have gas in the car." "I can't help that." That was always her go-to phrase.

You can only say that to a person so many times until they start to get it, and I feel incredibly blessed that I got it early. This is a lesson that continues to serve me well to this day. I learned to *not* allow my circumstances to dictate that which needs to be done. I accept that life is not always going to be easy for me, but then I hear my grandmother saying, "I can't help that." Not having a stable home, or father, or lots of money, or the newest clothes, had nothing to do with me mastering the art of reading, writing, problem solving, and building strong professional relationships. I realized it would be a little more difficult for me to do, but it wasn't impossible.

Two Things We Need To Change

I feel a sense of indifference has settled in with my younger brothers. Indifference can be seen in people that have an attitude of, "It doesn't matter. I can go either way with this." I get really angry when I perceive some of the things that my younger brothers are doing as indifference. Their mindset is: "It doesn't matter. I don't have to do it. I don't care."

First, we should change this thinking because *everything matters*. We cannot afford for things *not* to matter. There are people who can walk out of their house in pajamas and a tank top and go to the mall because their appearance doesn't matter to them, but that's not for you. It makes me angry when I feel and see that sense of indifference settle in on a community. I know what happens when apathy kicks in because I had that attitude at one time. It's dangerous when you don't give a damn.

When you don't care about you, it becomes impossible to sincerely care about other people.

You do not care about others feelings. You do not care about the path of devastation you leave behind you because you are busy satisfying your own selfish needs. You're only looking out for yourself. I've been guilty of that. It was very destructive. And this is particularly why it angers me when I see others doing this.

The second key point to changing the course for yourself, young brother, is to realize that none of us live or operate in a vacuum. We are part of a larger, interconnected community, and we each play a very important role. Knowing who you are at your core, and the type of leader you aspire to be, is part of the necessary self-discovery that real leaders intentionally make. Discovering who you are, what you bring to the table, what you're capable of, and the choices you're willing to make to get there, are keys to your evolution from naive boy to grown man.

Shake off the "I don't give a damn" attitude if it's descended on you. You want to be a "no-excuses" kind of guy. When you make a mistake, own up to it, and then keep going.

The day you stop believing that you can do something and you begin to rely on other people to do things for you that you're supposed to do for you, is the day you concede to not think on your own.

I cannot think of anything successful that I've achieved on my own. I certainly had support along the way. But *allowing* support and guidance is not the same as *needing* them to take care of me. I give myself permission to be amazing and rely on my circle of influence to guide me along the way. Just like in sports, your coaches coach from the sidelines but it's you that has to actually play on the field. I choose to play on the field of life and no longer worry about what place I will finish in. When I give myself permission to play, no matter what, I win. And this attitude has been the force behind me going on to earn a Bachelor's degree and three Master's degrees. The sky is the limit.

BIO

As a dynamic business consultant, best-selling author, and leadership development trainer, Alonzo M. Kelly has gained international and global attention as a premier consultant, strategist, and coach. He has co-authored two best-selling books with legendary leadership expert Brian Tracy and Jack Canfield of the *Chicken Soup for the Soul* series. He has appeared on "America's Premier Experts," which airs on major networks across the country including ABC, NBC, CBS and FOX. He is currently the exclusive executive coach for several large school districts across the country and senior leaders of Fortune 500 and 100 companies. He previously held the position of senior vice president and head of shared services for the Wells Fargo Funds Management group and led the operations of seven outpatient sub-specialties at the Children's Hospital of Wisconsin. He holds a Bachelor's degree in Accounting, three Master's degrees in Public Administration, Human Resources, Labor Relations, and Business Administration.

www.kellyleadershipgroup.com

....

2

Becoming a Champion
By Guy Whimper

To be a champion means staying focused, passionate, having dreams, a winning strategy, an ability to listen, avoiding bad choices, and being disciplined.

I studied psychology and sociology at the University of Minnesota in 1978. In 1980, I enlisted in the United States Marine Corps to serve my country and see the world. During my 21-year career, I had several jobs that included Drill Instructor, Hand-to-Hand Close Combat Instructor, and Platoon Sergeant for a security platoon in Operation Desert Storm during the Persian Gulf War. I served in Al Jubail, Saudi Arabia and in the desert near the Kuwaiti border.

I was married at 23 years old, and my wife and I raised four children: two boys and two girls. My second son, Guy Jr., played football. I encouraged it because I believe, like the military, sports are an excellent environment for learning values and lessons that help promote success in your life. You learn teamwork, organization, and how to execute a plan. You see the results of hard work and effort. You learn to understand motivation and determination. You also learn the six Champion Principles I share with you here.

Stay Focused on Your Dreams and Passions
Guy Jr. excelled in sports. He received offers from around the country to play basketball or football at Division I universities. He had the dream of playing professional football since he was 5 years old. I re-

member going through his stack of scholarship offers and coming across a letter from Yale University offering him a four-year basketball scholarship. I was ecstatic! However, he coolly informed me that he ran track and played basketball just to stay in shape for football. I had to remind myself what I had previously learned: *if a child has a positive dream, a parent should support that dream. The dream is the child's and not the parents.* I said to him, "But Guy, this is Yale. When you graduate, you'll get your class ring and start applying for jobs in corporate America. The interviewers will see your Yale ring and your credentials, and you will be a shoe-in as a new hire." We later find out he was right.

He became a professional football champion because he was passionate about it. He most likely would have been an average basketball player at the college level because his heart wasn't in it. He could have accepted Yale's four-year basketball scholarship, but basketball wasn't his passion.

So, he chose to stay close to home by accepting a football scholarship from East Carolina University. Then in his junior year, he became a father, but he didn't come straight out and inform us. I had to hear it from a friend of mine. When I asked Guy Jr. about this rumor, he confirmed I had a 2-month-old granddaughter. I asked him why he didn't feel he could come to us with such important news. He told me he was embarrassed because he was playing football and couldn't work to support his child like he had seen me do. He was seriously considering quitting college to go to work and support his new family. He was even considering joining the Army.

I sat him down and further explained my role to him as his father. As long as he was doing positive things, I would be there for him. Having a baby out of wedlock and before he was ready was not smart. However, my granddaughter was here now, so we gladly made adjustments. I commended him for wanting to sacrifice his football dream in order to be a responsible father. I told him it would hurt me to see him not pursue his dream.

He decided to stay and finish playing football at ECU. He ended up being drafted in the fourth round by the New York Giants as an offensive lineman. In his second year with the team, they won the 2007 Super Bowl. I will never forget that proud moment when I stood on the field with him as he hoisted the Super Bowl's Lombardi Trophy high up in the air. I knew he had fulfilled his dream – the same dream he'd had since he was 5 years old. I knew I had done my part. Guy Jr.'s journey reminded me about the power of focus. **Champion Principle #1: A champion stays focused and does what he is passionate about.**

Listen with Your Ears and Open Mind

My son learned that even though members of his pro football team made more money than the coach, they still had to listen to the coach and follow his instructions, otherwise the coach would sit them on the bench. It didn't matter the level of their talent. If they failed to follow instructions, they didn't play. They had to be able to, at least, listen enough to get onto the playing field. This holds true for any profession. Even the busiest CEO has to be able to listen to his or her customers. If the CEO doesn't listen, the customer doesn't use their product or service and takes their business elsewhere. The company then loses money.

Working with young people, I often see them challenged with receiving instruction or guidance. I see guidance and wisdom from the older generations being rejected because those of the younger generation believe they know best or think "my way is better than your way." In some cases, the younger person may have the better solution. But I believe in listening to all your options so you can make an informed and wise decision. However, in life, you don't always get the chance to ask for a do-over or to call a timeout to stop the action and assess as you would on the football field. As a young person, you have to listen to your coaches and mentors, develop a winning strategy, and hit the field as though your life depends on it because your life does depend on it. **Champion Principle #2: A champion listens.**

Avoiding Bad Choices and Influences

As a young teenager, I didn't *have* to rob and steal. I had a roof over my head, clothes, and food to eat. I chose to do burglaries and committed armed robbery *not* out of need but because of negative peer pressure. As humans, we want to belong, but I chose to hang with the wrong crowd. I always felt in my soul that it was wrong to rob and steal. There were warning signs showing me that I was on dangerous ground – being almost shot by the police, by homeowners, and in one instance by a jealous rival. I continued to run with my "homeboys" until I went to jail for theft. While in jail, I visualized my future. In that cell, I realized jail was not for me. I stopped hanging with my boys, and that was my first and last time in jail. **Champion Principle #3: A champion learns from his mistakes.**

Be Disciplined and Focused

I learned the importance of discipline and focus in Marine Corps boot camp. We were trained in skills that would help us survive on the battlefield. Being distracted by the chaos around you could get you or your squad killed. This holds true for you as you navigate through life. However, you don't have to go to boot camp to be instilled with these virtues and learn these types of skills.

A combat sniper may have to lay perfectly still in bushes infested with ticks and mosquitos and focus on a target almost a mile away. It takes extreme focus to make a shot like that. The point is to not let anything distract you from hitting your target. A professional basketball player makes the shot even when opposing players hit his shooting arm or have a hand in his face. If you develop this level of focus, it will help you be successful.

To me, self-discipline is means being able to assess your thoughts and actions then determine how they will affect your progress towards achieving your dreams. As a martial artist, I often visualize myself in various attack scenarios, and then I would envision how I would respond. If you were striving to become a lawyer, for example, you might visualize yourself defending a client against a particular charge. The key is to see yourself, in your mind's eye, actually doing what you love. **Champion Principle #4: A champion is self-disciplined.**

Realizing Your Dream

Every person has a passion, something they love to do – be it solving math problems, making music, designing clothes, playing computer games, or speaking up for other people. Consider this question: *If you had all the money you wanted, what would you get up every morning to do for free?* Your answer reveals what you are passionate about. Your passion is what you love to do and what you would be willing to do for free. When your passion is put into action, you are living your dream. When you are working on your dream, it doesn't feel like work. The money is not the motivation. It's just a nice addition; a bonus.

Once you discover your passion, you have to become a student of your passion. Study it; learn all you can about it and continuously learn. Don't waste time on distractions that will come at you daily. Use the Internet for research. A world of information is at your fingertips. You can also read books, watch how-to videos, read blogs, or go to free lectures in your city or on college campuses. Talk to those who are doing similar passion work. Seek out experts in your chosen field or passion. You can even ask one of those experts to mentor you. You might get together in-person or by phone on a consistent basis once a month or every other month. You can also ask to shadow them by going to work with them for a day or hanging out with them for a day observing how they do what they do. Ask them questions about their journey and what tools and skills they recommend that you develop to be successful. **Champion Principle #5: Champions learn from those who have gone before them.**

Have a Winning Strategy

A winning strategy is learning what you need to master to get to the top of your game and having a well-thought-out plan to get there. If the field you want to pursue is science, medicine, or engineering, there are certain math and sciences you need to study early on. If it is sports, music, or dance there are certain skills and techniques you must master. Whatever your field of choice, I recommend that you start preparing early.

It doesn't matter if you want to be a professional athlete, doctor, lawyer, truck driver, actor, skateboarder, painter, etc., they all require the same characteristics to succeed: self-discipline, a strong work ethic, focus, determination, and (equally as important) the ability to listen and receive instructions. **Champion Principle #6: A champion has a strong foundation, a plan, and a winning strategy.**

The Keys to Becoming a Champion

It can be to your advantage to get clear on your dream early in life. Then you can seek positive guidance on formulating a plan and begin to take action. Why wait? I am discouraged when I see young men shrug their shoulders and say, "I don't know," when asked, "What are you going to be when you get older?" The ones without a dream leave their life to circumstance, the will or whim of others. You want to be able to experience the rush of working towards being at the top of your game and fulfilling what you set your mind to do.

What I learned in boot camp, on the drill field, and during the time of war, and what my son learned on the playing field, can all be used in any career or business you choose. Just remember these universal characteristics of success:

- **Have a strong work ethic** – Put in the time with consistency.
- **Be self-disciplined** – Do what has to be done in preparation, being better, doing better, and getting better.
- **Determination** – Never give up.
- **Focus** – Stay locked on your target no matter what the distractions.

These will help you become a champion.

BIO

Guy Whimper Sr. is a certified life coach, military veteran and a counselor in substance abuse.

www.guywhimper.com

....

3

R.i.S.E. from the Darkness
By Claude E. McFarlane

This story, my story, is one of growth and accountability. Another way of saying this is: I had to learn to incorporate the principle of truthfulness into the decisions I made. Only by truly coming to grips with, and accepting the truth of, my life did I fully become accountable and begin to move forward in the proper direction. *So, what's real? What's the truth?* I had to learn through many painful lessons about the consequences of avoiding accountability, not taking personal responsibility, and trying to dodge owning up to the consequences and repercussions of my personal decisions and actions. Learning the power of being accountable is what led me from the darkness into the light.

Let me take you back… I was in Albuquerque, New Mexico a few years after college with my then-fiancée and our son when I found out that I had a 3-year-old daughter in Indiana from a previous relationship. I wanted to leave Albuquerque. I thought it would be best for us to return to my hometown of Milwaukee because my family was there and it was closer to my daughter. After a discussion with my then-fiancée, I got a job in Milwaukee and made the move. The plan was that she and my son would move to Milwaukee soon thereafter. Our relationship was a little shaky before I left and became weaker once I was gone.

She decided not to follow me and bring our son to Milwaukee because, honestly, I was not handling my business as a man. I was not focusing on and prioritizing her and my son. *A true spiritually-led man always prioritizes his family first and holds them as a unit to never be torn apart. He should serve as the foundation for his household and as a conduit between his family and God.* I was not that. I was not focused, didn't make the wisest of decisions, was not fully honest, and didn't portray a true spiritual man. This undoubtedly made her decision to stay in Albuquerque a lot easier because, despite how much I loved her, I should have never left without her.

I couldn't blame her for not following me, but boy did it hurt — *a lot!* I didn't face it — neither with myself nor with her. I turned to drinking. I turned to other women. I was not honest with myself or others. I lied because I thought, *telling the truth I wanted to live* was a lot easier than *facing the truth I was actually living.* I hurt the love of my life and lost her trust, along with the trust of some of my dearest friends and family. I wasn't fooling them. They saw that my actions were not lined up with what was coming out of my mouth. I was not practicing what I preached. I was not taking <u>full ownership</u> of my actions, nor was I consciously choosing thoughts, habits, processes, and people that would positively supplement my growth as a man. I still wasn't being accountable for my actions and selfish choices. I was still in denial with myself and with my soul.

Avoidance Does Not Equal Advancement

I have the gift of gab, so I literally would talk myself into the mind frame I *wanted* to have. I would tell myself that what I was doing was justifiable — whether it was partying, drinking, or being upset with how things ended with my ex-fiancée and trying to find a substitute by using women to fill the hole in my heart. I would simply ignore the parts of myself and my life that I didn't want to confront. I was just going through the motions.

As a result of having irresponsible sex, I found out that I was having *another* child...by a different woman. So then I had three kids…by three different women! I was *that* guy! I couldn't believe that I had become this stereotypical black man who had kids all over the place with different women. I knew in my heart that this wasn't me, but my life choices were saying that it was me. But I knew it wasn't what I wanted to be.

My situation was a fact, and I couldn't talk or justify my way out of it. I knew I was capable of more than this. I was having trouble finding my niche in my profession. I missed my first son. I wasn't truly being present in my daughter's life, even though she was now closer geographically. And my heart still hurts from my failed relationship with my ex-fiancée.

I was so out of alignment and had no principles to drive my character. I kept screwing up. I wasn't really changing my bad habits, and more importantly, I wasn't changing my spiritual compass and my mindset. I was frontin'. I would paint this picture that everything was okay so others would look at me and see an image of something I wanted to be, but wasn't. I wanted them to see the guy that had the engineering degree from Purdue and got the great high-paying job in sales with the prestigious company and would eventually be seen as a leader in the community and in his family. On paper, and externally, I looked great. But I was DYING ON THE INSIDE. And what you bury on the inside always eventually rises to the surface and comes out in some shape or form.

I was still in denial and not coming to grips with the turmoil in my life. I buried it instead of confronting it. I would cry at night and not sleep but for a few hours for days at a time. I had no drive, no passion, and no purpose. I lost my cushy sales job. I put on a façade during the day and was just miserable at night. I couldn't keep going on like this. It just wasn't natural to live life this way. I had to stop crawling in the dirt of the darkness and learn to breakthrough to the light of my R.i.S.E

Then a glimmer of hope appeared! I got a job after being unemployed for a few months. It was a large company, a visible position, and the money was great! I moved into a new place, had a great job, and had a nice car – things were looking up, *so it appeared*. As I reflect, on the outside it appeared that I was getting my life together, while on the inside there was still a huge mountain of things I had to deal with. I still didn't have closure on my heartache. I still was not cleaning up my habits and mindset. Spiritually, I was not aligned – though I had good intentions. I've come to realize that having good intentions doesn't justify lying and bad choices, nor does it really fix the mistakes of what is truly broken. Actions talk, words and intentions don't.

My Wake-Up Call

On February 6, 2015, at around 10 p.m., I was driving back to my new apartment on the freeway in my nice car with my new sports coat, bought with money from my new job. I felt like I was *finally* fulfilling the image of what I was *supposed* to be, based upon other people's standards and expectations. So I decided to go out for drinks with some of my buddies. I called myself celebrating the fact that I was a *new man*. Though the problem was I had too much to drink and then decided to drive myself home.

Ironically, on the drive home, I lost control of my car, spun out, and slammed into the guardrail totaling my car… on a bridge. I got a DUI and went to jail as a result. This was not the first time I'd had a DUI. I had to have my second son's mother, my mother and my sister bail me out. They were up all night worrying about me. My first son's mom was a co-signer on my car. Her credit was now shot, as was mine, because of my horrible decision to drink and drive. My bonehead decision affected not only me but my loved ones and the people who cared about me. There was a ripple effect happening there.

The DUI situation and car accident was a hard pill to swallow and brought me nothing but shame, guilt, and loss of faith in myself. And I was *still* thinking of how I was going to justify all of this and explain it to all the people I had to explain it to – *still* not being accountable and still not coming to grips with WHY it happened. I lost my job and my car because of this situation. No job + no money = no home. What was *this*? I hadn't figured it out yet, but it wasn't simply because of drinking and driving. It was something deeper. Claude still didn't figure out the WHY. Claude was too busy focusing on damage control.

Telling the Truth to Myself

I needed to get a grip and tell the truth (to myself and others) about what was IN me – about my confusion, shame, guilt, lack of closure, and being so upset with myself for some of the decisions I made over the previous three years. I was more worried about how to tell the story right so I could minimize the negative reflection on me as much as possible. I was worried about what my friends and my family would think. Here I was again trying to look good, please everyone else, and fill others' expectations of me, but not my own. This was part of what had me in this bad spot in the first place. I had no backbone, low standards, and no guiding principles for my life; thus, no character. I remember lying on my kitchen floor before I had to vacate my apartment. I looked up at the ceiling and cried out to God (damn near yelling at Him) and asked Him, "Why? Why me? Why all of this?" I heard no response, at least not then…

It wasn't until August 20, 2015, that I went to court and was sentenced for my DUI. I spent five days in the House of Corrections. That first night in jail, I just died on the inside. If there was ever a time in my life when I just gave up because I couldn't think of any other way out, that was it. I couldn't talk my way out of it. I was stuck and had to face the truth. No more self-justification and rationalizations. No more sugar-coating my poor choices and irresponsible behavior. Unlike me, I encourage you *not* to wait until you're at the end of your rope and feeling defeated and deflated before you own up to your stuff and start to be accountable for your choices.

I spoke to God. I cried to Him... without words. There was just raw emotion draining from my heart in between my muffled crying... And this time, He answered. I literally heard Him speak to me in my spirit. He said to me, "Are you done now? Have you had enough... of you? Are you ready to let Me be in charge?" And I said, "Yes." That was the beginning of my R.i.S.E. out of the darkness.

Here's what I had to realize in order to finally R.i.S.E. out of the darkness:

Re-Define and Re-Invent Yourself: Work through your past so that you can re-establish a better foundation for your future. You don't have to let what happened in your past or the mistakes you've made define you. Know where you want to be and start chiseling away negative thoughts, bad habits, toxic people, and inefficient processes. Be and live as the person you want to be, not the person you once were.

Inspiration: Once I began to R.i.S.E., I found the value of what was in me. I felt that the uniqueness and authenticity of who Claude was, was okay, and it was a good thing. That inspiration ignited the fuel of motivation to achieve my purpose. I was confident in my vision and finally focused on my future destiny more than on my past mistakes.

Spirituality: There is a seed of purpose that is planted inside of you by God. He knows the plans He has for you. If you try to go at it your own way and are stubborn in seeking Him, you undoubtedly will fall or have to take a longer or more painful route to your destination. You will struggle unnecessarily until you choose to surrender and be obedient to God's Word. The good news is that He will guide you to exactly where He wants you to be and you will abundantly be blessed!

Empowerment: Empowerment is the recognition, development, and execution of skill sets necessary to accomplish your goals. It also involves tapping the power that resides within you and leveraging your strengths to further shape and refine weaknesses or challenges that exist in your character. Embrace discomfort because you will never really know who you are until you're tested through adversity. Don't be afraid to take chances and fail. Just get back up again. Reflect on why it didn't work out, and then try it differently. Life can hit you square in the mouth sometimes, but you want to be resilient and bounce back. Challenge yourself to be the best you that you know how to be. You have it in you.

It takes faith, courage, resilience, and accountability to God's principles to stand firm in the renewal of yourself. Do not let others' perception of who you used to be, or their opinions of how you need to be, deter you from the pursuit of who you are supposed to be. Challenge yourself to R.i.S.E.

BIO

Claude E. McFarlane, Jr. went to Marquette University High School in Milwaukee, WI and studied Electrical Engineering at Purdue University. Claude has 12+ years of expertise in Business Development, Sales and Consulting, Engineering/Technology, Marketing, and Business Strategy.

He has worked in many areas that include healthcare, information technology, military applications, engineering design, and manufacturing across the United States with companies like Wheaton

Franciscan, GE Healthcare, Aurora Healthcare, Direct Supply, Sandia National Labs, Honeywell, and Boeing.

His life experiences, mixed with a yearning to execute God's purpose for his life, is what led to what he calls his R.I.S.E. – a method of personal enrichment and of how to live a life guided by principles. Claude has a passion and enthusiasm for speaking and leading.

Claude's mission and goal in life is three-fold:

1. Please The Lord God through surrender, faith, and actionable obedience.
2. Be an impactful man in the community and a great father to his children.
3. Fulfill his purpose on this earth.

He trusts that his passions and skills will pave the way of blessings for future generations.

www.mcfarlanegroupllc.com

....

4

My Dance with the Devil
By Dakarijon xRichardson

"To dance with the devil means to be influenced by negative actions or self-destructive behaviors that do not reflect your true nature nor create a positive future."

Changing your life can be a difficult task – this is a well-known fact of life. But as a child, I didn't really grasp the validity of this statement until it became directly applicable to me. As a teenager, I grew up in a fairly affluent, predominantly white neighborhood in northern Virginia. Growing up there heavily shaped my decision-making and the things I valued in regards to who I was and what my future would be. I grew up in a world where many of my black peers would try their hardest to "act black" by mimicking the rap videos and movies they saw on television. My white peers would expect me to act in the same contrived way.

With as much teaching and steering as my parents gave me about doing the right things, I still ended up finding out who I was, and what morals and values defined me, through trial and error. I followed my own path and had to face the consequences of that decision.

The Dance Begins
My "dance with the devil" began when I was 18 years old. I was leaving home to go to college, ready to experience real freedom for the

first time in my life. In high school, I hadn't taken my freshman or sophomore year seriously, which required me to have to put in twice the effort to improve my GPA during my junior and senior years. With an intense amount of concentrated effort, I was able to improve my grade point average from a 2.3 to a 3.4 within just two years. I realized that I couldn't make it into the college of my choice if I was going to continue slacking, so I began to dedicate all my energy to my school work. I spent every night, for a year and a half, doing homework and studying until 2 a.m. I wanted to ensure that my school work was the highest quality I could produce. My mindset shifted to being disciplined *now* so that I could prosper later.

My high school GPA allowed me to go to a decent school in Norfolk, Virginia. The transition from northern Virginia to living on my own in Norfolk was more of a cultural shock than anything else. The people I initially found myself surrounded by at Old Dominion University were from small country towns, which severely affected their mindset and world views. Innocent and eager to find my place within the school, I began to hang out with these individuals enjoying a life of partying and semi-mediocrity where average grades, goals, and aspirations were encouraged and accepted.

I began to slack off in my classes and became reclusive, interacting solely with those who were a part of the party world. My core values of education, self-improvement, and following through with positive action all took a back seat. I convinced myself that I had everything under control, while unknowingly letting my life slip through my fingers like sand.

I was able to maintain a C+ grade average by attending my college classes two to three times a week. But because I missed out on key lessons and lectures, I was soon lost. I slowly became depressed, unmotivated, and disinterested in my life and the world around me. I was self-conscious about how I was living, completely focused on the wrong things, doubtful about my ability to be a success, and insecure about my ability to truly reach my goals. As I allowed myself to become more and more entrapped with this new lazy and care-free lifestyle full of partying and sloth, the less focus I had on my priorities. I was dancing with the devil.

At that time, I didn't realize how large of a part my social circle and personal associations played in shaping my mindset. Growing up, I was taught that birds of a feather flock together. I was taught that who you associate with matters. *Studies have shown that we become like the average of the five people we spend the most time with. If you surround yourself with negative people, you will slowly become negative. If you hang out with five losers, you will become the sixth loser through association and the adaptation of group mindset.* I was so deeply entwined with these negative individuals that I had lost sight of my purpose and my true self. My life was falling apart. I felt like it was in shambles. I began to feel like there was no way out of my situation. My grades were slacking, my confidence and social life began to disappear, and my overall ambition, drive, and love for life had faded to become a shadow of itself. I fell into a spiral of darkness and depression. I call this *my time in the dark.*

Coming Out of the Dark

Eventually, I realized I had to stop when my life reached an all-time low. I woke up one morning and realized that I couldn't reach the lifestyle of financial freedom, extensive travel, and experiences I wanted being the person I was at the time. So I made the decision to change that very day. I recognized that I had dug myself into a deep hole, and it was time to pull myself out. I decided that I was going to live and die a champion, not a spectator. I was going to reach my goals, live a life devoid of fear and missed opportunities, and truly experience the beauty of life available to me.

A New Beginning

During my second semester of college, I refocused. I decided to stop dancing with the devil.

I started going to the gym, reading, and upgrading my social circle. My primary focus was on my academics. I slowly got my grades back into shape by shifting my life, attention, and energy back to the things that were important to me. I didn't just want to make an improvement; I needed to take control and lead myself back toward the life I wanted. I ditched the people who I had initially surrounded myself with and focused on absorbing and applying information through reading whether it involved learning about business, self-improvement, religious texts or meditation techniques. I was hungry to find any way I could to better myself.

Reading helped me expand my capacity to absorb new information and helped me shape my mindset to become more focused, goal-oriented, and ambitious. I began to exercise self-control concerning the people I hung out with, the things I did, and the women I interacted with. I became disciplined.

Every moment was spent reminding myself of the man I was trying to become. My grades went up drastically, and I could feel that I was truly making changes. Each day was an internal challenge to resist the temptation of going back to my old, mediocre, sub-par life – but I persevered and kept my eye on the prize. Over the course of a year, I put on 15 pounds of muscle, got an internship with Towanna Freeman at the Black Life Coaches Network, and raised my grade point average to a respectable and competitive level. I made a decision: I was done living my life like I was a passenger on a public bus with no direct control of where the bus was going. I wanted complete control and to take the steering wheel of my life in my own hands.

During my time in the dark, I began to realize my true value. I had allowed myself to become swept up in the chaos of life and peer pressure. I had lost sight of my prior ambitions and goals. The gradual formation and the strengthening of my values of strength, knowledge, and perseverance helped me not only develop my character but helped me become the man I am today. I had to learn to stop blaming external factors, such as people and my environment and look internally at myself with my strengths, weaknesses, and my own potential.

Associations

You want to associate yourself with people who not only hold the same values as you but who want to win, have aspirations and goals, and have the strength and determination to finish what they start. Every decision you make can make or break you or take your life in a very different direction. It takes a man of strong character to truly become a positive success in this world. A man of character takes control of his situations in life and strives to uphold and live out the values, morals, and ethics he holds closest to himself. He strives to maximize what he has and what he can do. As a young man, every day you're either building habits of character or destroying them.

Set High Standards for Yourself

When I began my turn-around is when I decided to set high and unwavering standards and values for myself. From the people I had to leave behind to the parties I stopped attending, every action I took was for massive, positive change and an upgrade of both my mindset and my lifestyle. Anything that didn't line up with my new, higher standards or where I wanted to be in life had to go.

I advise you to establish standards for yourself based on two simple questions: *Do you love yourself? Do you truly value yourself and your time?*

Whenever you're thinking of making a decision, you have to first consider whether or not it is lined up with respect to self and love of self. You also have to think beyond the immediate moment and consider the future.

Is an action worthy of your time? Does it align with the person you're trying to become?

Every action should be based on whether or not it arises from the best version of yourself. If it doesn't, take a pass because it's not consistent with your values. It's important to recognize and keep expanding upon the attributes that are important to you. Then come up with ways to improve yourself to become the best young man you can be.

Write It Down

The next step is to write out the attributes and values you wish to personify. Yes, write them down. You must evaluate your strengths and weaknesses with brutal honesty. This gives you a baseline for recognizing what you will accept and what you will no longer tolerate.

The next step is the hardest but also the simplest: take action. Far too often, people simply wish and dream about being better, but they don't take the actual steps to do it. It's the effort you put in *now* that you'll thank yourself for in the future. It is an investment that will continue to yield dividends.

Exercise Your Free Will Wisely

Remember, building character is about being wise in your daily life choices as well as with pivotal decisions that will shape and refine you into the man you desire to be. What you've been taught your entire life will affect your decisions, but ultimately the choices you make and the results you produce fall on your shoulders. The hardest concept to grasp as a child, teenager, or even young adult is that in this world you have the free will to do almost anything you want. You get to decide *what* you want, *how* you want to do things, and *who* you want to be. That's power!

You can always blame a lot of external factors for why you're not where you desire to be. You can blame it on your parents, how you were raised, your living conditions, or life circumstances. You may have even come out of a dire situation, but the one common factor and the common denominator in all these situations is *you.* As long as you're alive, you have the power.

Instead of responding out of triggered, knee-jerking emotions, you can decide to not *react* to situations but instead to *respond* to them. Ask yourself: *How can I build myself up to deal with the issues that beset me? How can I remain level-headed and think clearly?* Many times events are happening in your life, but it's up to you to decide HOW you will decide to view these events – either positively or negatively. You actually possess the power to determine what your perception is going to be IN a given situation and OF a given situation.

The legendary Chinese philosopher Confucius said, "The man who says he can and the man who says he can't are both right." The difference between where you are and where you can be is your mindset. Winners continue to win because their mindset is tailored towards their goal, while losers frequently lose because their attention is primarily focused on concerns about being defeated.

It's an everyday decision that you need to consciously make to improve on yourself, hold yourself to higher standards, and to hold your values high. No matter the outside pressures from society, family, friends, enemies, lovers, or mentors only you have the power to make your reality heaven or hell. What will you choose? Events will occur in life, and people will come and go, but it's up to you to decide how you will respond. Each positive decision you make will build on who you are and who you will become. Always remember, you have the power.

BIO

Dakarijon xRichardson is currently a sophomore at Old Dominion University in Norfolk, Virginia, studying business administration with a minor in international business. He has interned for personal branding firm Velvet Suite and life coach company Black Life Coaches. He has helped an assortment of brands and individuals find and improve their own unique personal style through image consulting and visual production. Dakarijon is an entrepreneur with aspirations to build his brand into a powerhouse that can help and inspire millions of people.

www.stylebynimbus.com

5

....

The Leader Within
By Taalib Boyd

My father passed away February 2, 1995, and I can still remember that day like it was yesterday. My father was one of the most influential people in my life. I was 10 at the time, so I transitioned into being a teenager without my father. That was definitely a difficult transition for me because my father was my hero. *He called me Ty.* His very last words before he passed were, "Tell Ty I love him." That was the type of connection we had. So when I lost him, it was a devastating experience that I vividly remember to this day.

I had to go through high school without a father. Growing up fatherless during high school in New York was definitely not an ideal situation. I never really had a good relationship with my mother, so trying to navigate through society in inner-city New York on my own was tough. I had to deal with the challenges that being an African-American male and growing up in that environment brought. I learned how you can go down the wrong path really quickly.

Eight years later, my mom passed away during my last year of high school. She became terminally ill, and as a result, she died. I knew that if I needed some kind of guidance, I could run to my mom. But when she died, I felt like a rug was snatched from under my feet. At that point, I had a certain level of numbness to her passing because every day I was living with the awareness that my mom could die from her illness at any moment.

However, my new-found inner strength came from exposure to new and positive people around the age of 16 years old, a couple of years before my mom died. I was starting to meet a new caliber of people who talked about becoming millionaires – who had big dreams. I started working a multi-level marketing business in the 10th grade. Although I was not successful with the venture, the business sparked a new excitement in me about personal growth. Where I'm from, you didn't hear conversations about success, bettering yourself, personal growth, wealth, and achievement. My ears and my mind were opened to this new world.

One piece of advice to you is: *get exposed*. Do your best to get exposed to new opportunities and new positive people as much as you can. Opportunities are everywhere. Stretch. Expand your thinking. Say "yes" even if it's new or different to you. Exposure helps with the decision-making process, and you don't feel as if you are being held hostage by one type of opportunity. A broader, personal vision is created by your exposure to opportunities that give you more options and expand your notion of what you can achieve in life.

I know I wanted more, but at the time, I didn't really see an avenue for getting more or achieving more besides the long shot of maybe playing basketball and hoping to make it to the NBA. I started to think, "Hey, I want to go into business. I want to own my own company. I want to be a millionaire one day." I had these dreams, and once I started to dream again, I started to realize that I could actually achieve some of these dreams. I started to believe in myself and not let anyone else define who I was. I was committed to *not* letting my past tragedies and the self-fulfilling prophecies of an underserved black child operating in an oppressive social-economic system confine my potential or impose limiting beliefs on me or my future.

Looking back, all that I went through gave me a strong sense of leadership. I have to attest to the fact that John Maxwell's *21 Irrefutable Laws of Leadership* is golden. Leadership is about having and using your influence. Influence is the ability to sway and affect circumstances and situations. The first person you must be a leader of is yourself. You may very well be the most difficult person for you to ever lead effectively and with consistency. My quest became to find out how to grow and cultivate that influence. Reading personal growth books and listening to audiobooks are some of the ways I've cultivated my influence.

I spend a good deal of time reading and listening to audiobooks. I'm definitely a John Maxwell fan. I listen to a lot of his books so I can grow my influence and use it to affect change in my community. *21 Laws of Leadership*, and *15 Invaluable Laws of Growth,* and *Rich Dad Poor Dad* by Robert Kiyosaki, are some of the books that greatly impacted me. If you aren't already an avid reader, I strongly encourage you to become one. Reading can open up whole new worlds of possibility for you.

I want to leave you with a few key nuggets of information that I hope will help you in your life:

1. Never let anyone define you.

In life, you will be constantly influenced by the things around you; from the billboards you walk by to the commercials you watch, the music you listen to, the social media sites you visit, and the people you hang around with and talk to. You must understand that, ultimately, you alone have to determine who you are.

2. Recognize that you are going to have two choices in your path to success and the pursuit of your goals: the pain of discipline or the pain of regret.

At some point, you're going to have to choose one or the other. If you want the pain of discipline, you've got to understand you're paying upfront and making a "down payment" on your future success. If you get the pain of regret, you're paying at the backend because of what you *coulda, woulda, shoulda* done or a poor choice you made. At some point, you're going to have to make that choice. Just choose wisely. I have often chosen the pain of discipline, and I've always been glad I made that choice.

3. Have a strong WHY when it comes to accomplishing your goals.

When you have many compelling reasons why you are pursuing a personal goal your reasons will give you strength when you come across adversity while striving toward your goals. When I was going through Air Force Officer training, my WHY of having more money with the position was not enough to get me through the training. I had to add more compelling reasons to help me develop the mental toughness to get through my adversity. One compelling reason I added to my pursuit was the reminder that people died so I could have the opportunity as an African-American to become a Commissioned Officer in the United States Air Force. So, I had to honor their sacrifice with my 100% commitment toward completing the training. Make sure you maintain a list of strong reasons of why you need to succeed in whatever personal pursuit you commit to in life.

4. Be cautious of your habits.

Your choices create actions, and over time, your actions turn into habits. Once that happens, those habits define who you become and how far you'll go in life. I always knew from a young age that I wanted to leave a mark of significance before leaving this Earth. I find it to be a real tragedy that many people live a life and die without ever pursuing their dreams. Oftentimes, people hit some adversity in the pursuit of their dreams and simply give up. They let their challenges shape their beliefs on what is possible in their lives to achieve. My CALL to you is to not be that person no matter what happens.

5. Make a daily decision to be your best asset in life.

We all have the choice to be our best asset or our worst liability. This decision must be a daily one. Every day I look in the mirror and make a conscious decision to be my own best asset in my life. With that said, being your best asset entails learning your strengths and weaknesses, while also dedicating yourself to growing in your areas of strength. It also entails finding others who can make up for your weaknesses as you build a team to help you achieve your goal as a leader. When I opened this chapter, I mentioned the first person you have to learn to lead is yourself. However, eventually, you must also learn to lead others to accomplish your dreams. All of us are leaders in some capacity, whether is in our family, amongst our friends, or in our own business. My humble opinion is that if you can accomplish your dream by yourself, then maybe you need to dream a little bigger. Be your best asset and grow that asset every day. If you grow in your areas of strength 1% a week, in about two years you would be 100% better than you are at your current best. My areas of strength I commit to growing in consistently are leadership skills, teaching, and public speaking.

What are your areas of strength you can improve in consistently?

Remember: Keep pushing forward, never give up, and never surrender to adversity. The world needs the gifts you have to offer. We are all counting on you, young brother.

BIO

Taalib Boyd served as a cornerstone contributor in the Continuity of Operations Program Development for the Long Beach Fire Department. In addition, Governor Andrew M. Cuomo has launched the Citizen Preparedness Corps Training Program, which will train

100,000 New Yorkers in the proper preparation for emergencies or disasters. The program seeks to provide citizens with the tools and resources to prepare for emergencies and disasters, respond accordingly, and recover as quickly as possible to pre-disaster conditions. Taalib has been a vital member of the training team for this mission.

Taalib also serves as president of Kaizen Strategies Institute, which provides leadership and personal growth training solutions around the country. He is also a keynote speaker on the topics of ambition, leadership, and dealing with adversity.

www.mrboydlab.com

....

6

Carpe Diem And The Hour Glass
By Matthew W. Horace

The sand in an hourglass reminds us of two things: how much time we've used and how much time we have left. Our legacies are created by the opportunities we are presented with and how we choose to use our time. Every sports coach I've ever had has pushed the idea that we are all presented opportunities to do something special in life and make a difference. I have learned that while we can see our life's time in the hourglass, life guarantees us nothing and we never really know when our time and opportunity will end.

I grew up in Philadelphia, Pennsylvania, watching young men doing time, wasting time, and on occasion making time. "Making time" refers to creating the life that you want and escaping the lure of the streets. In my neighborhood, I saw a full spectrum of people: middle class, professional, blue collar, poverty-stricken, hopeless, hapless, and young black men who never reached their goals and dreams because they become victims and perpetrators of substance abuse and crime. As a 15-year-old, I attended numerous funerals of friends who were killed as the result of senseless violence.

My mother is a loving pillar of strength. Her wisdom and encouragement inspired me. But she was also worried about how could she ensure that I would not meet the same fate as many of my own friends and classmates. She used to be brought to tears when she would read or hear reports about yet another young man dying too young. The narrative always seemed to be the same...a high school junior gunned down, stabbed, found, attacked, etc. I didn't understand her worry then, but I understand it now and am thankful for her concern and attention. She had many sleepless nights worrying that my fate would be the same as many of the friends whose funerals I attended.

My dad was committed to being present and an active participant, not a spectator, in parenting. The ultimate teacher and mentor, he preferred to teach me to fish, not just give me fish without showing me how to catch them. When I struggled with calculus, he would say, "Let's sit down and get this right." I hated it because he was a natural mathematician, and often I was tired and wanted to go to bed! If he was designing a project, he would say, "Come in here. I want to show you how to create a complete electrical circuit…" or change the oil on a car… or assemble a bike. His thought was that one day I might need the skills that he was sharing. Man, was he right!

I also learned very quickly never to tell my father that I was bored. When I did, he would take me to the library to become "unbored" with the endless list of possibilities that existed through books and reading. The message: there is much too much to learn to ever be bored. "If you are bored, pick up a book," he would say. My dad believed that his time was his ultimate contribution and that the time that he spent would create a legacy beyond his time on Earth. He taught me that everything takes time. Things that I wanted in life didn't happen overnight. They required time. To him, time was the most important thing in life. The hourglass was never half empty but always half full.

He also suffered from alcoholism for a brief period until he made a decision to quit drinking and made a full recovery. For the next 30 years of his life, he never drank alcohol again. His example showed me that he was always willing to work for what he wanted and that he could overcome adversity.

My parents' awareness and love inspired my focus and drive, and it lit the desire in me to become something more. Becoming something more would become an enduring principle throughout the different stages of my life.

Carpe Diem

"Carpe Diem" has been my mantra for over 30 years. It is Latin for "seize the day." If you don't seize the day, the day might seize you. The question is, do you want to seize or be seized?

I first learned the term in high school and became more familiar with its literary significance as an English major in undergraduate school. I was motivated to always want to do better and be more. I never wanted to be satisfied with the status quo. When I was growing up, I wanted more than a small row home, dirty streets, dangerous communities, and lack of opportunity.

As a teen, my challenges were like many other young black men in that environment: peer pressure and the lure of cool versus school. My friends were getting arrested for petty crimes and progressively serious ones. Several of them spent significant time in jail and several were killed. At least one of them was killed by police.

Many of these individuals grew up in households very similar to mine. They were just making bad choices and moving backward in life – standing still while their hourglasses ran out of time. In the end, their choices cost them their freedom, their imaginations, their innocence, and their lives. One poor choice on one day in one moment can change your life forever, and there are some choices from which you can't recover.

I had friends in every imaginable walk of life who were making bad choices. I was faced with the same choices. *Should I go left or right at that fork in the road? Should I gamble and drink beer on the corner, or should I go home? Should I take advantage of a female who has had too much to drink? Should I skip school and go to an arcade with friends, or should I go to the YMCA and to the library? Should I try an illegal substance at a party just this once?* I always felt that despite these influences, a more productive narrative with a different ending was possible.

Your fork in the road could appear on an evening in your neighborhood on the way home from school or when you are at a party and someone invites you to try an illegal substance. When a friend says, "I'm going to do this. Would you like to come?" Choose your direction wisely. If it doesn't seem right, it probably isn't.

As a young man, you will be faced with that fork in the road many times. *Each fork leads to a door; one door may represent dreams, and one door may represent doom. Which door will you choose? What types of friends will you surround yourself with?*

I had lifelong friends and role models, Keith Glover and Harry Cooke. They were the exceptions. They chose the path to success. I love and respect them dearly because they made positive, powerful choices.

I have always followed a relatively simple model: Follow those who success follows and success will follow you. On the other hand, there is the model: Follow those who are committing crimes and the police will follow you.

A Setback Can Become a Comeback

I have found that no one who has reached any measure of success has done it on their own or without setbacks. For example, as an athlete, injuries always set you back. As a freshman NCAA football player, I suffered a knee injury in spring football. I returned home, fearful of losing my scholarship, and had surgery. I recovered from the surgery, trained hard, and returned to school bigger, faster, and stronger. I initially lost my position as a starter and had to work to get it back.

During the summer of my sophomore year in college, I was bitten by a dog on my Achilles tendon, suffering yet another setback injury. I recovered from the injury, trained harder than ever, and returned to the football field bigger, stronger, and faster yet again. After each injury, I developed a warrior mindset. Although I was disappointed with my condition, if I couldn't run, I walked; if I couldn't walk, I did push-ups; if I couldn't do push-ups, I did sit-ups. When my access was limited to my home, I did 500 push-ups and 500 sit-ups on some days. I refused to allow anything to get in the way of my goals. Do not allow any person or condition to impede your goals.

Faith & Success

I also had very visible examples of success as I was growing up and as an adult. My great-uncle John Teagle, a barber and minister, is 87 years young and still cuts hair and preaches on some Sundays. He was educated in a one-room school in the Jim Crow segregated South. My younger brother, Michael Horace, is a successful Ivy League-educated architect. Both of these men are my role models in different ways, and I love, respect, and feel inextricably connected to them.

I am beholden to everyone who has ever placed their faith in me for any reason. My rent is paid every day to their faith and confidence and my ability to fulfill their positive expectations of me. A diverse tapestry of numerous great men, black and white, have poured significantly into my life.

I never imagined that I would have met presidents, gone to every state in the United States and many foreign countries, and investigated some of the most memorable and publicized crimes of our lifetime. I also never imagined that I would have been asked to provide commentary on law enforcement and Homeland Security matters on national and international television.

People who Made the Difference

Joey Jackson is a great mentor who helped me to dream. I never dreamt that I would give speeches to hundreds or appear before millions on TV networks such as CNN, HLN, NBC, CBS, ABC, the BBC (the British Broadcasting Corporation), and even on Philadelphia's NBC10 @ Issue news program on Sundays.

Willi Ellison, John Ross, Carson Carroll, Jim Zamillo, Jim Golden, Ron Nesbitt, Richard Kendell, Lewis Rice, Tony Torres, Mike Mason, Larry Ford, Greg Gant, Kelvin Crenshaw, Sewell Feddiman, Dave Sherman, and Coach Joe Purzycki all have inspired me greatly.

Every day, I want them to know that their faith was well-placed. I would not be the man I am today without their inspiration, guidance, and support. They taught me several things:

- Work is important, but family is more important. Real men take care of their families first.
- When things get rough (as they sometimes will) and the road you're traveling seems uphill, dig in, stand tall, and never give up.
- Build a network of advocates, sponsors, and mentors and allow them to help you uncover and actively share your gifts.
- Never refuse an opportunity now that might benefit you later. Accept additional responsibility as opportunities for growth, learning, and development.
- When you need help, determine who to ask, what you need, what you want the person to do, and ask for it.

Find someone who will encourage you to dream. When you execute your vision, everything is possible.

Mentoring

Young men need positive, strong male role models in their lives. I always saw my dad live by this. He taught me that, in terms of raising kids, you can't give them material things and not teach them anything. He never hesitated to tell me how proud he was of the father I had become. Though my Dad died in 2008, I will never forget the character he demonstrated while battling cancer for 10 years.

Mentoring and giving back is easy. I believe in mentoring for a lifetime. Giving back is like a mortgage payment for my lessons and blessings. I have both received and given. I have also led and been led by some of the most amazing role models and leaders on earth.

One of my mentors, a family friend and neighbor, was a veterinarian. Dr. Dean Hodges and his wife Barbara were shining examples of grace and success. They were both graduates of Tuskegee University – he a member of Alpha Phi Alpha fraternity and she a member of Delta Sigma Theta Sorority. They were examples for every young man and woman of the endless list of possibilities that one can achieve. I could have been a veterinarian because I saw that it was possible. I knew that he was an animal doctor before I could spell veterinarian. I decided to become a member of a fraternity because I knew that it was positive based upon my experience of Dr. Hodges. I saw Dr. Hodges several times a week in passing and a number of times each year because he cared for our family pets. His children and I attended school and played sports together. Dr. Hodges wrote reference letters for my college applications and was an employment reference for me. He even spoke with background investigators on my behalf when I became a federal agent. I am thankful to the Hodges family for being a part of my journey. Find someone to be an advocate for you, and be sure to thank them.

Four Essential Life Messages

The first message to you is to **live your life with enthusiasm and**

excitement. It is hard to be ignored when your shoulders are square, your head is up, and your eyes are bright. When you do this, your spirit will shine and people will be drawn to your energy. If you're shuffling your feet along on the ground with your head down, then it's likely that you are going to draw the attention of people who are doing the same thing.

Secondly, **live your life by design and not by default.** Don't just live, create a path and develop an intentional plan. Be sure to have a plan. Ask yourself:

Where do I want to be and when do I want to be there?
What are some of the obstacles I'll need to overcome?
What can I do, starting now, to better myself?
What are the actions and steps I'm willing to take to support my plans?
What are the results that I want to produce?

Lastly, I would encourage you **not to conform to anyone else's model of what success looks like.** Success is *not* one-size-fits-all. Success manifests itself in many forms and in many ways. A corporate suit doesn't define success and what success looks like. For you, it may be a lab coat, an architect's desk, having a business, a judge's gavel, or a microphone or paintbrush in your hand. All of our paths are different. Whatever your path, find it, be it and own it. Live your life with passion and purpose and one day you will say, "This is how I arrived. It wasn't always easy, but I got here. And it was worth it."

Finally, when you are able, **be that hand that reaches out and lifts others as others' have lifted you.** My favorite portrait is called "He Ain't Heavy." It was created by artist Gilbert Young and depicts an arm extended downward reaching for an arm extended upward. In your life, you will be both extending from and extended to. Your joy will come as you lift others up and provide access to success. Remember, access for one can mean access for many.

BIO

Matthew W. Horace is a senior vice president for a national security firm in New York City and a former federal law enforcement executive. He is a sought-after media contributor to national news networks, an author, a motivational speaker, and an adjunct university professor.

He is a member of Phi Beta Sigma fraternity, president of the 100 Black Men of New Jersey, and a life member of the National Organization of Black Law Enforcement Executives. He is also an advisory board member of the Federal Enforcement Homeland Security Foundation, a consultant to The Hetty Group, and a member of the Black Life Coaches Network.

www.matthewhorace.com

. . . .

7

You ARE Good Enough
By Nicholas Dillion

The Formative Years

I was born during my mom's seventh month of pregnancy and weighed a little over two pounds. As a result, my lungs did not fully develop, and my immune system was compromised. I developed asthma at 7 months old and faced a series of health challenges as a child.

During my elementary school days, I was terrorized in the classroom through bullying and ridiculed by my peers for not being able to participate in a lot of recreational activities. By age 15, which I consider my impressionable years, I started feeling like I was reaching my breaking point.

I could not understand why I had to be sick or why I was required to deal with a medical condition. I felt that I was being prevented from having my full childhood experience. I often felt alone in my world and even created myself an imaginary friend so I had someone to talk to. My days consisted of me going to school and then straight home with no ability to participate in any extracurricular activities such as basketball, football, or soccer. My respiratory system was not strong enough to withstand the physical activity. Plus, I was on daily medication and was required to use a nebulizer breathing machine every four hours.

I grew up with three other brothers who were reasonably healthy. Because of that, I would have a big ole pity party on a daily basis. Unfortunately, technology wasn't as advanced as it is now for me to connect via the Internet with others like myself. There were times when I didn't think that I would make it to see age 21, let alone 18.

My health condition created this very dark and isolating place for me. I started battling with depression at age 15. This caused me to become reclusive, withdraw from my family, and become very introverted. During those times, in the African-American community of Milwaukee where I was raised, it was taboo to reach out and seek the help of a counselor. It was unheard of to go and talk to an outside professional about your personal challenges or issues, to share thoughts on your mind or heart, or to share the truth about what was really going on inside your home.

You were encouraged to speak to the elders of the family or your local clergy or pastor. That was it – but not a professional. So, with these limited options, I chose to simply keep things to myself and just tried to deal with it. My trust level with my parents was not great, and going to someone outside of the family never crossed my mind.

Being one of four boys growing up in a household of very strict parents, I was very resistant to speaking up or sharing my feelings and emotions about anything because it meant I was *less than a man*. I believed I needed to be strong, emotionless and *hard* in order to be accepted. I picked up on this by watching my brothers and others in the neighborhood interact with each other. To me, it seemed my parents were on autopilot and parented based upon the premise that (as a child) I had no voice and was not to have an opinion. To challenge or disagree with my parents was never an option. They made sure we had food, clothing, and shelter; were educated and went to church. Anything else was not a priority. I often felt as though they did not love me.

It was challenging for me to connect emotionally with both of my parents. I could connect with my mom as a nurturer because I was sickly, but it was a challenge for me to connect with my dad emotionally, especially since he was always working. He was the provider. He went to work every day and when he was home he was only there physically. When dad came home and my mom said we were disobedient, we were disciplined. By disciplined, I mean whooped with a belt. Because of this, I rebelled a lot. I would refuse to talk with him or speak to him because he was intimidating and emotionally unavailable. So, I avoided him at all costs. I wanted nothing to do with him. I felt as though the only connection I had with my dad was a bad one, and that devastated me. I literally hated him.

This caused me to become withdrawn at home by not wanting to socialize or participate in family functions. And when I went to school, I was bullied. But, what I found as solace was listening to music and going to church. Church actually became my safe place. When my mom took us to church, I felt the love there along with a unique sense of family. Church filled my emotional void, and it is where my mom and I grew closer.

One of the things that I knew I could count on was going to church on Sundays. We also went to Bible Study class on Wednesdays. The knowledge that was being poured into me was amazing. I didn't realize what good it did me until years later.

Church was a place I could turn to, and it can be a place of comfort and support during challenging times for you too. If you don't have a church or a support group, find one.

Writing My Way Out of Depression

Living through constant hospitalization, all the while navigating through the turmoil of school bullying and my home life, was tough for me. At 15 and a half years old, my life got so dark that I contemplated making an irreversible decision. I thought to myself, *what is life offering me right now? I'm sick. I don't have a whole lot of friends. I hate it here at home. I don't think my parents love me. I don't think my brothers like me. I can't get along with anybody at school, so why should I stay?* I decided that my life was not worth living, and my best option was to end it.

One lonely summer afternoon, I decided that this was the day. I went into the basement, and I decided I would end my life. My plan was to go and hang myself in our basement. I started out to do just that. The saving grace for me was due to a protocol in our house. When mom called you, you had to answer immediately. She also needed to hear your actual footsteps walking toward her for her to know that you were quickly coming to see what she wanted. On that particular day, as I was in the basement getting ready to string the rope over the pipes that ran overhead above the washing sink counter, she called me. I answered. Then my mind went to the thought, *I need to start walking because she needs to hear my footsteps.* I went upstairs to see what she wanted, and I never returned downstairs.

I am unsure of what transpired over the course of the rest of that day. I may have very well deleted it out of my mind. However, I do remember that after that incident, I began pouring myself into journaling. I had heard about girls writing in diaries at that time but hadn't heard of boys writing in diaries. So, I simply used a notebook with no lock and put it under my pillow. I started writing on a daily basis as a reflection of my feelings and thoughts. I even recall writing a poem about death. I felt like I had no outlet with other people; plus, my journals didn't judge me as I felt other people did.

I would definitely encourage you to get a journal and begin writing in it. Start with what you're feeling; do it without judgment. The written word is a form of expression; it is transformative and provides you with an additional tool to find and express your own voice. When you utilize free-writing and allow your thoughts to hit the page without editing, you can notice things about yourself that you may have never stopped to realize. Your thoughts become clear.

Your fears, worries, and concerns can be poured out in a way that you might not otherwise have the space or the bravery to admit verbally. You can even experience some relief from the release. Just write the truth from your heart.

Finding Myself

When I graduated from high school, I received a scholarship to Marquette University. Actually, of us four boys in my family, three of us received scholarships to Marquette. With regard to education and discipline, my parents were on point with this. However, when I got to college, I was still in this place of trying to find myself. I was still not really comfortable in my own skin. I was still struggling with just being okay with me. I took all of my childhood feelings of insecurity and inadequacy to college with me.

Believe it or not, I actually met my future wife in high school. We were friends while in high school, and our relationship developed further while I was in college. Her upbringing was completely opposite of mine. She experienced mental and emotional abuse. So, here we were – two broken individuals entering into a relationship with lots of emotional baggage. By broken, I am referring to challenges with self-image, confidence, and self-esteem. We both depended on each other for lots of validation. We were not prepared for the family struggle we were undertaking and the challenges ahead.

Whenever there was a disagreement with my wife, I felt myself reverting back to how I felt at home with my parents. I didn't have a voice. I was feeling stifled, alone, and less at peace. Why? Because I still was not really rock solid and comfortable within myself. Because of that, I recognized that I had to do a whole lot more work on me. What I was doing was not enough. I did not want to raise children to be a reflection of what I disliked about myself.

As much as we loved each other, we still had real life problems. I became a dad at 21 years old. We married at 22. Then, two additional kids came into the picture. We then had a household of five, and I had to be the ultra-provider. What I knew about being a provider was that you went to work, you paid the bills, and you came home. I didn't know how to emotionally connect with my kids at all. I just thought that if I was physically present and was providing that I was doing my due diligence.

What I didn't realize was that I was modeling what my father had shown me, only to realize from conversations with my wife that this wasn't working. My family needed me to be more engaged, and I needed to be physically present as well as emotionally engaged and connected.

We often find ourselves sometimes in the midst of being like our parents. The key is to being aware so you can make necessary changes.

Loving Yourself First is Essential

I worked hard to instill this in each of my children. I love me first and that love has transcended through ongoing self-care, allowing me to love my wife of 25 plus years the way she needs to be loved.

Although I am in a different space in my life now, I still have to work on myself. That's why I'm so passionate about ongoing growth. It's important that you keep learning every day. Continue to read books on personal growth and development. I would recommend my book titled *Who Do You Think You Are? - The Power of Believing in Yourself*. I would also recommend *Let it Go* by T.D. Jakes, which is another amazing book on moving away from the past and embracing the future ahead of you. Remember you are never alone as God is always with you. Surround yourself with positive influential people who want the best for you in life.

Growth and development allow you to keep getting better. As you keep getting smarter, wiser, more resilient, you will be able to navigate through life with a stronger and more expanded mindset.

You will be able to deal with challenges more confidently and more effectively. Personal growth and development provide you with a competitive edge in the corporate world, in business, in your relationships, and in your life in general. It separates you from those who are only *book smart*.

Think of a seed that is planted with the hopes of growing into a big fruit tree. It cannot grow if it has to totally rely on the rain 100 percent of the time. It takes more than just water for the seed to germinate and grow into a healthy fruit-bearing tree. At some point while it is young, someone has to care enough to take the time to water it and protect it from weeds, bugs, and other things that might stunt its growth or choke its roots. As it grows, it still needs to get pruned so it can continue to look full and refreshed throughout the year.

Well, just like the fruit tree, you too need ongoing nurturing and development to stay refreshed. You need to have a daily regimen of positive self-talk that allows you to be mindful of your thoughts as they drive your behavior. You need to believe in yourself. You must recognize that you have limitless opportunities to be the highest expression of yourself that you can be.

You are good enough. You are good enough. You are absolutely enough.

BIO

"Inspirational," "Innovative," and "Empowering" are but a few words to define the character of Nicholas Dillon. An entrepreneur in his own right, Dillon is on a mission to pursue his passion and build a legacy of influence.

The Milwaukee native possesses a Bachelor of Arts in Communication and a Master's in Adult Education. He also holds a Master of Science in Counseling. He is currently pursuing doctoral studies in Behavioral Psychology. Dillon's career has placed him in front of business professionals all over the world, including appearances on national television. This experience and growth has allowed him to join the John Maxwell Team of professional speakers and leadership trainers. As a No. 1 best-selling author, professional coach, consultant, and radio personality, Dillon has a limitless future and is a mogul in the making.

www.nicholasdillon.com

. . . .

There is Hope
By Dr. George James

Growing up, my family and I had a lot of love, humor, and faith; but, we did not have a lot of money. My parents are from Jamaica and moved to the United States with the hope of having a better life. My father didn't complete middle school because he had to take care of his younger siblings. My mother didn't complete high school but attempted to get her GED when she came to the United States. She failed the exam by a few points and never went back to take it again.

Although my parents struggled with formal education, they are very intelligent people nonetheless. I saw my mother create a financial system to manage funds as the church treasurer. Not only did I notice her intelligence but her integrity. Even if we were on our last dime, she would not be tempted to take or use any of the church's money. On the other side, I would watch my father attempt business after business. He was an entrepreneur at heart with many clever ideas, but he was unable to gain the success he desired. Thanks to the work ethic of my parents, I knew at an early age what hard work and sacrifice looked like. How could I not learn from such great examples?

I Will Do It By Myself

I grew up in North Jersey. In my sixth-grade year, we moved from Teaneck to Hackensack. In Hackensack, there was everything – celebrities, business executives, people who worked in New York City, wealthy families, blue-collar families, low-income families, families living in the projects, and people from the Caribbean, Central and South America. The poorer part of town was across the train tracks where families were working-class, middle-class, or in poverty. There were people who also "lived up on the hill" in huge houses or in high-rise condominiums overlooking New York City. Regardless of income, everyone attended the same schools together.

One particular day in the sixth grade, I wanted to buy lunch but was short a few dollars and asked a classmate for money. I remember him saying, "Can't you afford your own lunch?" I was embarrassed. I did not know if he said this because I was new, black, because my family had less or all of the above. It was then when I realized I was different. I was wearing sneakers from Payless while others wore higher-end name brands like Nike, Reebok, and Adidas. In addition, I had just moved to a new place and was trying to figure out who my friends would be. Lastly, being a first-generation American with Jamaican heritage, I sometimes felt that I did not fit in culturally. I believed that my classmates perceived me as less than them because I couldn't pay on my own. As a result, I made a decision to not feel that way again. *I was not going to ask people for anything anymore.*

What decisions have you made to avoid feeling negatively based on your perception of how others view you?

Help is There, Waiting for You to Ask

Ten years later, while I was in my master's program, I was confronted with a decision. Dr. Swint, my clinical supervisor, said, "George, you know what your problem is, right? You don't ask for help." I replied, "Yes, I do." But when I reflected, I realized she was right. I had a negative association with asking for help or even being vulnerable enough to admit that I could not do it on my own. This statement from my supervisor created a shift in me because it allowed me

to realize that I could not be as successful as I wanted without asking for help.

From that point on, I actively sought out mentors and others I could learn from. When I look back, I recognize that even though I thought I was operating on my own, there were key people – like Drs. Nance, Collymore, Keita, Lucky and Lafferty, professors from college, Mr. Johnson (counselor at the Drop-In Center at Hackensack High School), and Mrs. Jackson (my African-American and U.S. History teacher at Hackensack High), who were always there for me even when I was too stubborn to ask them directly for help.

For instance, the night of my prom, I spilled something on my jacket before the limo picked me up. Upset and frustrated, yet not knowing what to do about the spill, I went to our pre-prom showcase. When I arrived there, without me asking, Mrs. Jackson immediately comforted me and helped me remove the stain. I went on to have a great prom night with my date and classmates.

Who do you go to for help?

Who is already helping you but waiting for you to ask directly for more help?

Many young men struggle with asking for help because it requires vulnerability to accept advice from someone who knows more than you. Many young men fail to realize how many people are truly invested in their success and might be willing to help if asked.

Sometimes, we stop interacting with people who could help us because we try to avoid feeling ashamed, embarrassed, unloved, abandoned, or rejected. I thought I could control the outcome by not being vulnerable enough to ask for help. But, that also kept me from learning more about life, school, sports, and more. My reluctance to ask for help and seek out mentors became a blind spot. For instance, it kept me from playing high school football after my freshman year because I did not want to ask others for the help I needed to excel (because football was new to me) nor did I want to interact with the new coach who seemed difficult.

What's your blind spot?
What is really keeping you from asking for help?
What areas do you need help in to excel?

Success Requires Sacrifice

My parents made many sacrifices, including denying themselves opportunities they deserved for my education. They often said, "We want you to do better than us. We want you to go to college." That encouraged me to do well in high school and score high on my SATs. So when the time came, I applied to seven colleges and was accepted into all seven. I narrowed it down to my top three choices: Georgetown University, the University of Pennsylvania (UPenn), and Villanova University. After an interview process, I received notification from Villanova that I received the full-ride Presidential Scholarship. If I decided to attend and accept this scholarship, it would pay for everything including tuition, room, board, and books.

At the same time, I received great financial aid packages from Georgetown and UPenn that combined both need-based grants and merit-based academic scholarships. The packages at these schools were great, but I would still have to take out student loans. I thought about going to UPenn or Georgetown because of the names and prestige. Even with the option of going to college for free, my parents still insisted, "It's your choice." They were willing to do whatever it took, sacrifice after sacrifice, to enable me to be successful and realize my dreams.

Accept All of You

Sometimes, we think we can escape difficult feelings such as shame, embarrassment, or rejection. Not so. Without knowing it, choosing to attend Villanova would cause me to face issues of shame similar to my middle school experience. I thought that college would be a fresh start. I worked throughout high school and could buy my own things. I made friends of all cultural backgrounds and felt I was on the same level as others.

By the end of my first semester, a friend gave me a watch for Christmas. It was unexpected, especially since she and I were just friends and I was in a relationship with someone else. It was a Movado watch (I knew nothing about Movado at the time). It was easy for me to become skeptical and think, "People like me, who come from where I come from, don't give out $300 to $400 gifts to 'strangers'." It became clear there was a difference between her family and mine. This time, I was not going to let potential differences impact me like they did in the sixth grade. I had to make another decision – not to reject or devalue my financially humble upbringing. *All of my experiences (good and bad) make me who I am and I am okay with all of me.*

Can you appreciate that everything about your family, neighborhood, culture, race, friends, and income make you who you are today?

Can you embrace what the lessons of shame, embarrassment, and rejection have tried to teach you?

Can you accept all of you, including your positive and negative experiences?

- Start accepting all of who you are today.
- Embrace that you are more than your negative experiences and more than your less-than-ideal circumstances.

- Everyday, tell yourself, "I AM SUCCESSFUL!"

Every Experience is A Gift

All of my positive and negative experiences, including embarrassment and feeling different from others, provided me gifts – gifts like empathy (acknowledging other people's feelings because I could acknowledge my own feelings) and perception (being sensitive about my views of someone else or paying close attention to subtle details). Being empathic and perceptive were gifts that helped me to become a good therapist. Everything that you have been through and are going through now can be used to fertilize your life and to make your life better. **It is all a gift.** Once I was able to see what I experienced as a gift, I was able to use it to help myself and others.

Your experiences with money, no matter how much you have, is a gift. Your racial and cultural experiences are gifts. The sacrifices made by the people who love you are gifts. The people who are already in your life trying to help you are gifts. Each gift provides hope for you and your future. You dream for a better life, just like I did. **All of these gifts will help you realize that there's hope that things can and will get better.**

You can Achieve Your Dreams when you:

1. Stay hopeful.
2. Recognize You Cannot Reach Your Dreams on Your Own.
3. Ask, Ask, and Ask Again For Help.
4. Pay Attention to Your Blind Spots.
5. Make Sacrifices Because Success Requires Sacrifice.
6. Accept All of You – the good and the bad.
7. Remember That Every Experience is a Gift.
8. Never Stop Dreaming & Never Stop Pursuing Your Dreams.

BIO

Dr. George James counsels, consults, coaches, and teaches people how to overcome everyday relational struggles to build successful connections in love, family, and career. With a practical approach to relationships and life, Dr. James helps bring success within the reach of those he influences. He is a licensed marriage and family therapist devoted to helping people improve their quality of life by being involved in the healing of their wounds and enrichment of their relationships. Dr. James has been a recurring expert guest on many radio, TV, and online programs. In addition, he is a reoccurring contributor to Ebony Magazine. He also works extensively with professional athletes, adult men, and young adult men on various issues – including defining manhood and career and work-life balance.

Dr. James is president and CEO of George Talks, LLC, a communication and consulting company. He is a staff therapist and AAMFT-approved supervisor at Council for Relationships. Dr. James is also the program director for the Couple & Family Therapy Program at Thomas Jefferson University. He is married to Candace, and they are parents to their beautiful daughter, Nalani, and cheerful son, Alexander.

www.GeorgeTalks.com

....

9

No Matter What, You Can
By Seth Henderson

Inception

I was born in Harlan County, Kentucky, which is about 150 miles from Martin County, Kentucky, where President Lyndon B. Johnson visited in 1964 to bring awareness to poverty in America. Nearly 30 years later, I was born, and the pervasive chains of poverty still weighed down on many people born unto a place without a choice. I am proud of my roots, regardless of the poverty that prevailed, because they have shaped my character and ability to empathize with others.

I was raised by a single mother. I have a brother who is four years older than me. My father left the picture in my early teens. He was far from a role model. I still struggle with trying to remember the last time I saw my father's face. My mother and brother had always been the people who cared for me and loved me, so when my father left the equation, it wasn't a huge blow. I got all the love that I needed from them.

My mother decided to move us to Berea, Kentucky, when I was in middle school, and this was the beginning of a really stable period in my life. I was able to go through my last year of middle school in Berea and then on to high school. It was not until my final year in high school that I decided to go to college, and I eventually became the first in my family to do so. This was unchartered territory.

Unchartered Territory

Deciding to apply to college was solely my decision. I wasn't pushed to make that decision nor was going to college an aspiration that was expected of me. I in no way blame anyone, because being college-bound was just not something that my family had been exposed to. So I made that personal decision, honestly out of witnessing the difficulties that other people experienced who did not expand their horizons beyond the area they were born and lived. I wanted to broaden my horizons and expand beyond what my upbringing had exposed me to. I honestly believe that one's place of birth or your ZIP code should not determine your outcome or opportunities in life, but unfortunately, too often it does.

So I attended Eastern Kentucky University, about 15 miles from home. It was nice to be away from home, but it was also nice knowing that I could easily go back home to spend time with my mother and brother. At that time, I had no idea what I really wanted to do professionally. I just knew that I really loved the complexities of the criminal justice system. Initially, I wanted to become a cop and then work for the FBI.

Once I got into college, I worked diligently to maintain a good grade point average. It was difficult the first couple of years because I did not have the luxury of reaching out to my mother or brother to ask them for guidance on college or how to navigate it because I was a first-generation college student. Again, this was uncharted territory, so I had to rely on myself for many things and learn.

Although the first couple of years were rough getting used to, they were good. Then in my sophomore year, I met a professor in one of my criminal justice classes named Dr. James Wells. One day he approached me after class and asked, "Have you ever been interested in any student organizations? You have the highest grade in my

Stats class, and I just wanted to know if you were interested in any-thing. If so, I will help you get involved in an organization."

With that simple question, I felt my worth was affirmed; I re-ceived validation from a male figure in my life — something that was severely lacking. That moment was the inception of a new relation-ship. Dr. Wells is very much a person I consider a father figure in many ways. He encouraged me and helped me to release the poten-tial within myself that I did not recognize I had at the time. The key to the realization of my potential at that time was affirmation and confidence given to me by a respected male father figure. His sup-port and his belief in me and my abilities gave me the confidence to push myself even further out of my comfort zone of shyness, which had paralyzed me for much of my life. So I worked and participated in some student organizations.

My first victory in college came when I decided to run for a leadership position within the Golden Key International Honor So-ciety — the student organization for which Dr. Wells was the adviser. I took a leap of faith and decided to run for president of Golden Key, and to my astonishment, I won! Over time, I went on to lead other student organizations and to create a mentoring program to decrease the chances of freshmen dropping out of college.

My mother had already instilled greatness within me, a strong work ethic, perseverance, and integrity. In my opinion, I have the best mom in the world — to me, she filled the shoes of two parents. However, having that encouragement from Dr. Wells and him telling me that I could do anything I desired was the reason I was able to accomplish so much in college.

Outside of my mother, and before Dr. Wells, no one told me that I could do it. No one had spoken to me with such belief in me and my abilities. I think a lot of people just need to be told they have value — that they have a spark within them to do what their heart de-sires; that they have what it takes. And eventually, like myself, it gave me the courage and strength to take control and guide my future. Great potential is within all of us; however, the key to unlocking this greatness lies within you and hinges upon your attitude.

By my sophomore year, I decided that I did not want to become an FBI agent. Instead, I got the political bug in school and fell in love with campaigns and the political process. I got an internship with my local congressman and gained my first real exposure to the grassroots level of campaign organizing. It was exhausting but rewarding, and I loved every moment of it, fighting for policies that I believed were fair and just.

New Possibilities

In my junior year, I set out on the path to acquiring my Ph.D. I wasn't sure in what area but maybe public policy or sociology. I became aware of a program at my university called the McNair Scholars Program named after Ronald McNair, the African-American man who died in the Space Shuttle Challenger explosion in 1986. The McNair Scholars Program was created to encourage minorities, first-generation college students, and students from low-income backgrounds to pursue a Ph.D.

Becoming a McNair Scholar opened up a whole new world of possibilities to me, and I was introduced to academic research. Then I decided that I would like to do a research fellowship at a different school, so I applied to this oppurtunity called the Leadership Alliance. It was a consortium of top Ivy League schools, and they gave you the option of picking which school you would like to apply for; you were able to pick your top three choices. I applied, and I chose Harvard as my first choice. I was certainly not expecting to be selected, but one thing I have learned over time is *if you don't ask for something, you'll certainly never get an answer.* So I applied and was accepted into the Leadership Alliance's Harvard Research Program! I learned that you should never say "no" to yourself until you ask and give someone else the chance to possibly say "yes" to your request. It was an incredible opportunity where I studied the racial implications of DNA collection in America.

While in Cambridge, Massachusetts, where Harvard is located, I was introduced to another amazing opportunity that had the possibility of taking me to our nation's capital. The McNair Scholars Program emailed me information about the White House Internship Program. This potential opportunity meant that I would spend my last semester in college working in the White House and serving the president of the United States. I quickly realized that many interns came from well-connected political families, more affluent backgrounds, and Ivy League educations. The idea of interning at the White House had never crossed my mind, and I knew that if I decided to pursue this I had an uphill battle. I began researching everything possible about the program and the candidates that were commonly accepted. It was clear to me that I was not in the best position to be selected. On top of the odds being stacked against me, this was also an unpaid internship. But, I decided to apply anyway.

Back at school, I let Dr. Wells know that I was applying, along with some other mentors. The application process took about four months, but I also wanted to prepare financially just in case I was accepted. I knew that if I were to be accepted into the White House Internship Program I would face another hurdle, and that was the financial aspect since it was an unpaid internship. Having come from a single-parent household, I did not have the money to sustain myself living in Washington, D.C. without any income. Plus, it is an expensive place to live. So I reached out to another mentor at my university, Allen Ault, the dean of the College of Justice and Safety where I was working on my criminal justice course work.

Dean Ault asked me, "What do you need? How can I help you?" And I told him, "I have not even been accepted yet, but if I were to be accepted, I'm going to need some financial support from the university. So he said, "Okay, we will meet with someone from the university board." What eventually happened continues to amaze me even to this day, and I revere it as a major blessing. Before I met with a member of the board, Dean Ault told me to prepare a proposal of financial items that I would need if I were to live in Washington, D.C., for a semester. Dean Ault, acting as the father I viewed him as, walked with me into the meeting. We sat down with the board member and had small-talk for several minutes. Then the board member asked me, "What is the magic number you will need?" I told him my magic number, the dollar amount that would cover each of my expenses. And he said, "We'll get it for you." I'll never forget that moment. That moment was something that elevated my confidence to new heights. Dean Ault was actively supporting me and vouching for me. It was a surreal moment, and I felt like this was meant to happen. The financial burden on my shoulders was lifted with those five words. All of this was before I was even accepted into the program. Fast forward a couple of months, I received the email that I had been waiting months to see. I was accepted into the White House Internship Program to serve under President Obama's administration! This was certainly a once-in-a-lifetime opportunity.

After living in our nation's capital, I returned home to graduate from college. After I graduated, I knew that I wanted to be engaged in the campaign process. Luckily for me, Kentucky had an exciting Senate race that presented a great professional opportunity, so I volunteered to work as an intern. Eventually, I was hired and gained the professional grassroots campaign experience I desired since college. Once the election ended, I was introduced to another opportunity – to work on President Obama's My Brother's Keeper initiative, which was created to address the growing issues facing boys and young men of color in America.

You Never Lose, You Keep Learning

I have learned in my 25 years that the term "family" extends far beyond blood. I have been fortunate to have people appear in my life at pivotal times who loved, encouraged, and supported me; and took on support roles and mentor type capacities that gave me the strength and courage to take chances and believe in myself. If you're from a disadvantaged background, it can be especially hard to actually see the possibilities unless someone shows it to you, tells you that you can do it, or gives you the affirmation, guidance, and support that you need.

Everything that I have accomplished was not done alone. It is impossible and naive to embark upon a journey alone and expect to be successful. You have to decide NOT to let your circumstances define you and change your character.

I believe that if you work smart, not hard, and try to seek out new opportunities without getting comfortable with the circumstances or conditions that may be around you but step out of your comfort zone, the world will open up to you. You will see things that you have never seen before.

My story and circumstances are not unique and are similar to many across this country. We all have unique experiences and challenges that shape our character. Remember, you can choose to have a defeated attitude, or turn the challenge into a tool and a stepping stone to help you break down obstacles and move forward. There are many definitions of character; I believe that it is in our basic human nature to desire to improve ourselves, and it is this internal force that enables us to rise above our challenges.

I believe in you. No matter what, you can!

BIO

Seth Henderson has a record of serving others, which was galvanized as a first-generation college student. Born in Harlan County, Kentucky, Seth has demonstrated that one's place of birth does not have to determine one's future. He attributes his accomplishments and work ethic to his mother, brother, and mentors. Seth was a double major in criminal justice and political science at Eastern Kentucky University. He is a McNair Scholar and former White House intern for President Barack Obama. He is also a former research assistant at Harvard, where he studied the racial implications of DNA collection in the criminal justice system.

Public service and politics are his passion. He has worked on a Senate and congressional race in his home state. Currently, he works on a project called My Brother's Keeper Alliance, an initiative implemented by President Obama. The goal is to make the "American Dream" available to all boys and young men of color by eliminating gaps in their opportunities and outcomes. He believes that helping others is a moral and economic imperative. He currently resides in Washington, D.C., and serves as a Youth Advisory Board member of the In a Perfect World Foundation.

seth.henderson2014@gmail.com

. . . .

10

"The Good Life"
By Keith Willis

Finding Myself

If I could tell it my way, growing up in my world was tough. I was a military brat and every few years I was moving around. This meant I never could get settled in one place without wondering how long I would be there. When I was about 15, we finally settled in Norfolk, Virginia, but it was a different type of environment than what I was used to.

Living on a military base was safe. All of the kids were kind of the same. All the parents were the same. And then, all of a sudden, I'm taken away to a city with a lot of different people from different backgrounds that didn't grow up quite the same way I did. I grew up in a military household, which meant growing up in a very structured and disciplined environment. The kids in this city were raised differently than I was; not that it was better or worse, just very different. So not only was this a geographical move, but I had to make major changes socially.

As if being the "new-kid-on-the-block" wasn't bad enough, I was also the new kid who was becoming the star athlete in both football and basketball. Because the people in Norfolk loved sports, I dealt with jealousy from the guys. I was looked at disparagingly because, as they saw it, I was taking other players' playing time and attention from the media. On top of all of this, I was also dealing with the challenges of learning who I really was. Women started to catch my attention. Here I was trying to manage being a teenage sports star, but I had no idea of who I was as a young man. *Who did I want to be? Who was I at my core? What type of identity did I want to have?*

I felt like I was constantly having to work on trying to be accepted. Life was already confusing and wanting to be accepted brought pressure with it. I would often wonder, *"Should I act this way? Should I dress this way? Should I look this way? Should I do these things?"* I was always questioning and doubting myself because I knew a lot of things that I wanted to do didn't align with how I was raised. For instance, skipping school or smoking were some of those things.

Around the same time, I was exposed to alcohol, drugs, sex, and all of the things that were considered "cool." I never experienced these things before, but I knew if I wanted to be considered cool or accepted, I had to do these things. I also knew if I did, I would have problems at home. That's where the conflict came. And this is where things got worse.

I feared my parents more than I feared my peers, to say the least. My mom and dad didn't play any games. Also, I knew even at that age how much, especially my mother, had poured into me. She wanted me to be successful and I didn't want to disappoint her. I knew these things I was wrestling with wouldn't lead me to success. My ultimate goal was earning a college scholarship for basketball or football and then going on to play professional sports. In my gut I knew that the things I was struggling with "out in the world" wouldn't lead me to that. Things that I was being taught at home was more aligned with achieving my goals – so it was home that won.

When you are conflicted with what path to take, whether to listen to the outside voices of friends and society or not, if the choices in front of you support your future, move forward.

Pressure

I encountered several situations that made me more mindful of the negative choices I found myself making. There was a time when I got in a fight. Well, one of "my boys" got into a fight and he caught the worst end of it. Naturally I wanted to go and get the kid that beat him up. After the fight I remember thinking: *It doesn't ever stop because now they'll come back and look for us.* This thing never stops. I remember at that point, thinking to myself, *This isn't what I want to do.*

Besides fighting, the pressure I was feeling to have sex was intense. It was the thing to do as a popular athlete. I had virtually unlimited access to girls but I wouldn't have sex at that point quite yet. One of my good friends got somebody pregnant and I saw what it did to him. It caused him a lot of extra stress and financial strain on both himself and his immediate family. There was a lot of stress and fighting with the baby's mother. I remember thinking: *I don't want that.*

This was a constant struggle that I eventually gave into because I wanted to be accepted by "my boys" and be one of the cool guys. At one point, I thought I had somebody pregnant in high school, and it scared the living daylights out of me. This girl thought she was pregnant and my first thought was, *"Oh my gosh, now my career is going to be ruined. I'm not going to go to college now."*

In that time period, if you got somebody pregnant, everything was ruined. The pregnancy scared me to the point of almost paralyzing me. I vividly remember what it did to me and that feeling of dread and having to face my parents. I thank God that she wasn't pregnant. That alone was enough for me to get myself together. I didn't want that feeling *ever* again.

When you feel any pressure to do something that could jeopardize your future, think twice. In a blink of an eye, one poor decision can change your life forever.

Facing Challenges Alone

I received good leadership from great coaches and teachers. But interestingly, no one ever spoke to me about the issues in my life. Maybe because I hid it well. Maybe because I was known as a good guy. They probably assumed I had my stuff together. So they probably assumed I didn't need that help. The truth was: Regardless of appearances, I needed it as much as anybody else because I struggled internally with being accepted.

I remember I was going to fight and there was this older guy that had graduated two years previously. He was what you'd consider cool at the time, and he said to me, "You give me something to brag about. Go ahead and focus on sports. Give us something to talk about out here on the streets. Don't worry about this. We got this." At that point, I remember it stuck with me. To me, he was saying, "Keith, focus on your gifts. You don't have to run the streets to try to fit in."

I finally realized that I could just be myself and do what I loved to do. That was good enough to be accepted by my peers. That was a defining moment in my life.

What is something that you're good at that you can focus on instead of trying to fit in? Being yourself and doing what you love, I learned, is key.

Goals

One of my big goals was to get a scholarship offer from the University of Michigan. When I received an offer my junior year in high school, I realized that I was doing something right. I was on the right path. That football scholarship offer was huge for me. Then signing my scholarship to Virginia Tech was another moment when I felt I made it. I reached a goal. I signed a scholarship to play both football and basketball at Virginia Tech.

Another big moment for me was to try and graduate with both my bachelor's and master's degrees from Virginia Tech. Everybody's used to getting their first degree and then the other, in sequence. However, I set my sights on getting both in the same time span while I was still on scholarship. That was pretty cool – having a master's degree at age 23.

When all the basketball and football scholarships started coming in, I started realizing I was wanted and needed at these universities. I didn't allow the things that were going on around me, the hating from some of the people that I came across, the fighting, the temptation of drugs and alcohol, to affect anything. I knew exactly where I was going. I knew I was going to be playing on TV really soon. It changed my perspective on what was important at that point in my life.

When you have goals in life, everything else should fall to the wayside. It is how you accomplish what you set out to achieve.

A Change In Perspective

With all that I experienced I came to realize that the things I initially thought mattered, didn't matter anymore. For instance, needing the acceptance of certain people and feeling I had to partake in certain activities to be cool. If it didn't help me get to the collegiate ranks or put me in a position to do well, I know that I didn't need to be a part of it.

I also now believe the "good life" means that you're doing what God called you to do. In the past, I was under the influence of other people's thoughts and opinions, so when I pictured the "good life" it was about how many women I had, how much money and material things I could accumulate, and being recognized in public. I now believe walking in your purpose with God is the "good life."

Your goals should be geared toward putting yourself in the position to do what you purpose is on this earth, whatever that may be and to stay in alignment with that. It's about operating in your gifs and allowing those gifts, desires to open up doors only you can walk through. If what you are doing only benefits you, that's not God's vision, it's your vision. Your God given vision have you serving a lot of people beyond you. You are just the one he chose to steward the vision. To me, that is "the good life".

BIO

Keith Willis is a native of Norfolk, Virginia. He attended Virginia Tech on a football scholarship and also played on the basketball team. Keith graduated with a Bachelor of Science degree in 2003 and a Master's degree in 2004. After college, Keith went on to play in the NFL for five different teams. After transitioning out of the league, he started a wellness training company, Untapped Fitness, where he incorporated personal training with corporate wellness programs. Along with being a businessman, Willis also created a program to help high school football players prepare for the sport at the collegiate level. After working tirelessly for seven years, Keith switched careers and launched the MOSS Movement, a life skills company that helps athletes respond better to adverse situations off the field. His career has taken off since incorporating public speaking.

www.mossmovement.org

. . . .

11

Breaking the Cycle
By Corey Graham

High school was the point when I finally came to grips with the fact that my dad was never going to be around. It was hard to accept. It was critical for me to face the facts. My dad came to visit when I was 7 years old. I didn't realize that it was the last time I would ever see him for many years. He had voluntarily left me and my mother's lives. Once I got to high school, it hit me and it hit hard. It was a very bitter pill to swallow. It was a very challenging thing to deal with because I never received an explanation for his early departure. As I got older, I realized when I looked within, that I had a void – a void that only my dad could fill.

Identity Crisis
With dad gone, I was left with the daunting task of finding my identity as a young man. Mom, a soldier in the military, taught me discipline, respect, and the value of having a strong work ethic. She maintained the household in such an amazing way, providing so much wisdom to me, but from a woman's perspective.

I remember entering into school with so many unanswered questions about my dad. I developed so many insecurities, so many doubts, at a time when I was very, very susceptible of attaching myself to virtually anything that would make me feel needed, respected and appreciated. I was very confused.

I was involved in sports, but there was still a part of me that yearned to be accepted. During many games I'd look over to the sidelines imagining what it would be like to see and hear my dad cheering me on when I shot a layup, scored a goal, or made a tackle.

What did I do? Did I make him leave? What's wrong with me? Am I not good enough? I must not be that special, if even my own dad doesn't want to be around. These were the messages and questions that plagued me every day.

Outside of my home I was vulnerable and easily enticed by activities that went against my mom's standards, searching for validation. I had few friends who had both parents in the home, whether it was step parents or their biological parents. For the most part, we came from single-parent family homes in my neighborhood. A lot of my friends felt and experienced much of the same thing I was going through, so it was not hard for us to get into trouble. I easily got involved with people who liked to steal, drink, smoke, fight, cheat and disrespect women. I had nothing to lose, because what I felt mattered to me was lost.

Getting into trouble and getting involved with "low life" activities was our way of trying to deal with the hurt. When you're numb, or when you're trying to avoid feeling the pain inside of your heart, you're quick to latch onto those things that seem to alleviate the pain temporarily.

Subconsciously, I didn't even realize that, on the inside, I was thinking about my absent dad, "This is my way of getting back at you. This is my way of making you pay." But what I didn't understand is that the consequences of my negative "get back at you" choices and behaviors fell upon *my* shoulders.

Face the Void

If you are like I was, you might be dealing with this too. Maybe you're not doing well in school, and you struggle with being able to express what's going on within yourself. I encourage you to acknowledge, identify and name those feelings that you are experiencing. I think it's also important to address the mental and emotional road blocks that you have created or encountered. You have to be very specific with it.

Face the void that has been created as a result of your dad not being there. Courage and vulnerability are essential because you are going to look at places within yourself where it may feel dark, sad, lonely, and even terrifying. You are not alone.

Inside that void there's desperation for love and acceptance. But that need for love and acceptance can be held captive by pain. Pain is something we will try to avoid re-experiencing at all costs. Similar to a cancerous tumor, if you don't address the pain and the disease, it only continues to spread and cause further damage to you.

Particularly with us young men, we tend to express one emotion very easily: anger. This can potentially be very violent and create life-threatening situations. It can cause us to make hasty decisions out of emotions or reactions instead of thinking it through, instead of being level-headed, and also without considering the consequences of our actions or reactions.

For me, I had to be able to name the emotion and say "Okay, I feel resentment," which is accumulated anger. Not only was it toward my dad and within me at this particular point, but it started to show up in other areas as I continued to grow up. Academically while in college, I continuously dealt with questioning my ability and feeling inadequate, which later brought on tremendous amounts of anxiety. It required counseling, medication, and learning coping mechanisms to get through. Professionally, I questioned myself a lot and did not embrace my natural leadership skills with confidence. So, I pursued comfort and stability instead of greatness.

Determine, Decide and Move Forward

My mom got married when I was 19. I was pretty hard-headed because I was so angry at the fact that my dad wasn't around that I sort of made my step dad pay for it. When I went off to college is when it really settled in. I realized, this man was here to stay for the long haul. Sixteen years later, my mom and step dad are still together. This is powerful.

If this is also your reality, there are things I've come to accept that have helped me move forward in my life and they may help you too. I encourage you to remember this:

1. Acknowledge and accept the fact that your dad may never return to your life. If possible, seek out the reason(s), especially if you are dealing with the assumption that you're the cause for his absence.

2. Your dad's absence is not an excuse for your behavior. If you are being disrespectful, disruptive, and following the wrong crowd or engaging in criminal activity, that's your decision and you need to take ownership of it. I've heard too many times, "I have anger and trust issues because my dad was not around." That may be true, but it doesn't give you the justification to make others pay for what someone else did to you. It's important to not use this as a crutch, or an excuse for why you feel the way you do and for why you continue to act out in a certain way.

3. Determine and decide upon the man you will become. This is a chance for you to develop standards in your life. For me, as a result of his absence, it motivated me to decide that I would not become a dad until the right time in my life where I was able to take full responsibility and commit to being present in that child's

life forever. Be the generational curse eliminator. This is your opportunity to break the cycle, which will create a positive trend in your family and community.

I Don't Need Help

Every male authority figure I encountered in my life up until age 17, to be very honest with you, I hated. I didn't even have to know him well. If you were a male, and you demonstrated some type of authority or leadership, I hated you. In my mind, it was because you were trying to be something that I never had. Because I was angry, I was going to make your job very, very difficult.

I remember early on my mom tried to get a few mentors in my life, a few men to step in and be that, not necessarily a father figure, but just to be a friend, a big brother. I remember these potential mentors would come by the house and try to visit. I never answered the door. I remember them ringing the doorbell, standing on the other side of the door, knowing I was home and just hoping that I would answer the door. In fact, it became easy for me to reject these outreach attempts. I already had a wall built up. At that time in my life it seemed far easier to be mean, combative, and disrespectful than anything else.

Things started to change when I met a man by the name of Sanford Greene. I pay him so much respect because of his approach. I remember Mr.Greene because he was very persistent in trying to help me. He challenged me by asking me a question: "Corey, how much longer are you going to run?" He saw right through that, and he said, "Look man, you have one foot in and you one foot out." Nobody had ever asked me that question like that. I also remember him following up and saying, "I'm not going to chase you. Until you are ready to decide, then I'm right here."

He pushed me to start having some truthful conversations with myself. What that did for me was put the responsibility squarely back in my lap. It put the decision back on me at 16 and 17 years old. I had the decision to make. *Was I going to settle for living a negative life that was constantly rationalized by the fact that I didn't have a dad around?* It was at that point that I started going to church and really started to try to turn things around.

I really had a hard time dealing with my anger, and so one of the things I would do is write a lot. I started to ask myself some of those very tough questions and write down my answers. *How does remaining angry and bitter add value to your life? Are you willing to miss out on having great relationships with others because of his absence? Are you ready to free yourself of this pain by letting go?* I also started to have conversations with my mom, asking why my dad was not around. She really started to break it down to me as to why he wasn't present.

Pursuit of Peace

When I saw my dad for the second time after 26 years, it was my chance to forgive. I was 33 years old, married, and living in Charlotte, North Carolina. He was visiting my family in Georgia when my uncle called and suggested I speak with him. Toward the end of our brief conversation I invited him and his family to visit me anytime. You could hear the excitement in his voice and he agreed to do so. His wife prompted him to leave Georgia and come to Charlotte to see me. In less than 24 hours my dad was standing in my driveway.

I was able to courageously stand in front of him. At that moment I experienced what it was like to extend forgiveness to someone. I saw this 50-plus old man walk up to me, repeatedly saying, 'Corey, please forgive me. Please forgive me.' In response to his plea, I hugged him. I said, 'Wow, this is what it's like." I did just that, I forgave him and that was the final release to peace. What happened in the past no longer mattered, and the assumptions of his absence were no more. The lessons from my step dad, Sanford, and a host of mentors prepared me for this moment. This reunion between Dad and me didn't make up for 26 years of absence, but it provided me the chance to let go of the past and end the generational curse of not being reconciled with my father. When I forgave, it meant no longer bringing up the past to him, releasing anger, and being willing to build a relationship from this moment for the rest of our lives. I was no longer filled with the need for retaliation, but reconciliation. My responsibilities as a man are on my shoulders, and I cannot use the absence of my father as an excuse. I was no longer living to fill a void, but instead, to build a legacy.

I had finally broken the cycle.

I still remember every bit of the feelings during that phase of my life as a fatherless child. I now work with and speak to fatherless boys in similar situations as mine, and the same questions are still being asked. The same feelings are still being felt. I'm still seeing the same facial expressions, the same mannerisms and body language that I once displayed. This tells me that this is an epidemic that has gone on way too long. It's very cyclical, and I'm constantly working to figure out ways to end this cycle. This is why we must learn to forgive to break the cycle.

BIO

For the last two decades, Corey has demonstrated a relentless commitment to delivering inspirational and thought-provoking messages. As a teenager he gave his first speech about life growing up without a father. It was at that point that Corey embraced speaking as a purpose. Corey is the co-founder of The M.A.D.E. Company, which is a personal and professional leadership development firm with a focus on leadership, coaching and training.

As a founding member of the Queen City Toastmasters Speakers Bureau, a member of the National Speakers Association, and a Competent Communicator (CC) through Toastmasters International, Corey has continued to strengthen his ability to reach a diverse audience, serving as a catalyst for those who want to reinvent their lives. He is a graduate of the University of North Carolina at Charlotte with a Bachelor's Degree in Business Management. Corey has also completed the Fundamentals of Co-Active Coaching through the Coaches Training Institute, the John Maxwell 360° Leadership Training, and is a Certified Customer Service Professional (CCSP) through The Training Bank and the Customer Service Institute of America. In addition, Corey was recently awarded the Certified Coaching Professional designation from the Center for Coaching Certification.

His professional background includes experience in sales, management, financial services, operations and project management, and work in the nonprofit education reform arena. He continues to feed his lifelong passion for service as a case manager/coach for a male youth violence prevention program, which serves young men in middle and high school.

www.themadecompany.com

....

12

It's Possible

By L.L. Leonard

Over the past 25 years, my colleagues and clients have referred to me as "L.L," instead of Le'Detrick L. Leonard, it was easier to say. I grew up in a household with my mother and younger brother. Although my real father wasn't involved in my life consistently until I was an adult, I had a stepfather who was in my life until I was about 13. My stepfather would still come around periodically due to the fact that he was my brother's biological dad, but he and I never regained a relationship from that point. I had too much anger and hatred in my heart toward him because of the things that had been done to my mom and me.

After their divorce, I became the man of the house very quickly. I excelled in academics and in sports, and I went to college on a scholarship. But the negative impact, I guess, of not having a father around, not having positive role models around, adversely affected me.

I had a hobby of cutting hair and that was how I helped support the family and paid for minor things I needed for school. My mother normally worked 3 p.m. -11 p.m. or 11 p.m.-7 a.m. throughout junior high and high school. That left my brother and I home alone most afternoons and nights. This also meant that after school and practice I would come home, check my brother's homework, do my homework, either warm a meal up my mom made or create a meal so that we could eat. Then, start it all over the next morning, getting both of us up and ready for school.

Often, there were times that the physical, mental and emotional abuse from my stepfather impacted all three of us emotionally and mentally and it was hard to function at a normal level. As a result, the three of us had a very hard time trusting any male figures that tried to come into our lives.

I personally became resentful and very angry internally. My brother became very withdrawn and began to act out at home and at school. This caused him to drop out in middle school.

The three of us turned to experimenting with drugs and alcohol in efforts to self-medicate the pain. This resulted in a series of bad choices that led to a run-in with law enforcement for me and my little brother. My mother fell deeper and deeper into depression, mental illness and substance abuse. The alcohol and drugs she used made her check out a lot of times from being a parent. So there would be weekends where she wouldn't be around, and it would just be me and my brother. This pattern continued throughout high school until I had a minor break when I went to college.

I was excited for that opportunity to get away to a whole new state, excited about having my education paid for, excited about sports, also a little relieved of the responsibility that I had for so long. But then when I went away, things became really, really worse for my mom, my brother, and with the finances. My brother, who was about 13 or 14 at the time, began to get involved with bad people and making bad choices. He also became a teenage father with no income, no job skills, no education, no guidance, no parental support, and no real direction.

My friends and family would write and/or call me while I was in college to inform me of the incidents. This hurt my heart tremendously. It also made me feel very guilty because I felt it was partly my fault because I left him by going to college. There were many times when food, shelter, finances, and basic needs were hard to acquire. In addition to this, I also suffered a bad sports related injury that threw me into major depression. I made some very poor decisions that got me into some legal issues. And I also had a child on the way at 20 years old. The combination of these events happening at the same time compelled me to come back home.

Well, when I got back, I was such an emotional wreck. Here I was, with a promising career as an athlete/academic and now it was ALL OVER. I had to return back to my old neighborhood that I despised so much and the source of a lot of my pain as a child.

I had to return to the very house that I vowed to never return to again. I had to deal with the insecurities of feeling like a failure. I felt like I had let myself down, my mom and brother down, and my community down. I now had to face the harsh reality of coming back to support myself and the family in any way I could. I went through times where I just wanted to check out, meaning that I didn't want to deal with anybody or with life. I felt bitterness, resentment, frustration, disappointment, and anger. I was angry at God, at the world, at myself, at my mom for sure, and deeply disappointed in my brother because, at that time, he had a baby on the way at age 14 with no education or means to support this new life.

So I got involved with partying, abusing alcohol, dating a lot of women, and all sorts of destructive behavior. I was doing everything I could to be emotionally "numb" so I could function ... so I thought. My goal, subconsciously, was to do whatever it took to mask the agonizing pain that I felt in my soul ... to the very depths of my spirit. But it wasn't helping me move forward. I still felt alone, misunderstood, neglected, not cared for, hurt, frustrated, confused, disappointed, and angry at the world.

I now had felony convictions to deal with, child support due, a gambling addiction, a number of dysfunctional relationships with many women, and illegal activity. Many of these situations I feel like

I wouldn't have been in had I been mentally and emotionally more stable at that time. I was in desperate need of some positive male figures in my life to give me guidance.

Real Manhood

Around age 27, I started actively seeking out a church. I felt that I needed a faith-based community with a strong community of men that I hoped would help me in some kind of way understand how to process all of this. Although I had my skepticism and doubts about church, I knew that I needed something greater than myself to help me transform my life. I also knew that I could not do it alone. I was going to need the support of others. So I returned to the very faith in God that my mom had instilled in us early in life as kids. I needed God to be my source of redemption and transformation. I began to visit different churches and attending Bible studies in hopes to get some very much-needed answers for my life's circumstances.

Now that I was a business owner of a barbershop and a father, I knew that I couldn't keep living the way I was living and still be respected in the community and as a leader of other young men. So it took a few years to get myself together. I guess my early 20s and mid-20s was a difficult stage. And then when I got into my late 20s and early 30s, things started to kind of settle down, and I began to mature and understand real manhood.

The Road To Healing

It took many years of grief, and a lot of therapy sessions dealing with myself, my anger, and my resentment toward my mom for the many times she deceived us, broke our trust, manipulated us, disregarded her responsibilities as a parent, and made us feel abandoned and neglected.

She basically gave up on being a real parent after her relationship ended with my brother's dad. I also I had to forgive my own father for being absent for so many years – this too made me feel un-protected and rejected. I had to eventually forgive my stepfather for his many years of verbal, physical, mental, and emotional abuse to-ward us. I wasn't able to forgive until I sat down with a therapist that had me write out this long "burn letter" and read it to my mom.

A "burn letter" is a letter expressing all of the painful memories that one can recall from early childhood, all the way to current. The receiver of the letter's only job is to listen while you read it.

Upon completion, you are to ask permission to read it to the person(s) that you feel is the source of your pain … without interruption. After reading it, you are to burn the letter completely. As the ashes ascend toward the sky … so is your pain (metaphorically).

It was an emotional roller coaster having to recall some of those in-cidents. It took me several days to finish writing the burn letter. As I wrote, it there were so many gallons of tears pouring out from the depths of my sea of hurt.

When I was able to pour out my spirit, pour out all the pain and the resentment and stuff that I remember from 2 years old on to my mom, I could feel my release and healing taking place. And for the first time in my life she didn't make excuses, she didn't blame, she didn't try to project it on something else. She just listened to me and said, "I'm sorry." I knew that she had taken some responsibility for the impact of her choices upon me. This was the beginning of our new relationship. Once this happened, our relationship changed and was able to grow in a different way because I felt she was finally taking responsibility instead of insisting that it was somebody else's fault.

That's when a light came on for me. I knew there were other young men that were affected in the same way I was, growing up without a father, and/or having abusive parents. I knew there were other young men like me who had their development as men stunted and interrupted by the pain in their lives. They didn't have someone to help them navigate through those rough patches in the road to manhood.

I decided to start mentoring young men and connecting with other men in any way I could serve them. My barbershop was the perfect atmosphere for men to be comfortable enough to be vulnerable with one another and to get the support they needed. Then I started officially coaching and mentoring young men, public speaking and volunteering. Soon I realized that it wasn't just young men that needed support and healing in their lives, but men of many ages.

It's Possible

I believe the No. 1 thing I try to impress upon my mentees is that *IT IS POSSIBLE*. Regardless of your circumstances, regardless of your upbringing, your mindset, whatever it may be, IT'S POSSIBLE.

It is possible for you to overcome the pain in your heart from childhood. It is possible to be very successful in life, regardless of how unfortunate your beginnings may or may not have been. It is possible to find healing in your life by forgiving others who may have caused you pain. It is possible to reconnect with the purpose and passion that God has placed in your heart for your life. It is possible to be redeemed from any harm that you have caused yourself and others. It is possible to forgive YOURSELF for any bad choices and disappointments. It is possible to be a positive influence on other men by sharing the experiences of your life's journey.

Whether you come from an abusive background like I did or a loving and stable background where you had your parents around, whether you were great academically or athletically or not, it's possible to live a better life. And the way you build that life is to allow other men you trust to help guide you on this journey. I encourage young men to seek out men that can understand your path because someone has traveled a similar path before you. Someone has walked that journey already. You are NOT alone.

I will leave you with this:

1. It's OKAY to be "confused." It's okay to not know, and it's okay to not have it all figured out. And even though we have egos and testosterone that get in the way, sometimes you have to be willing to acknowledge the fact that really, you just DON'T have the answers. I want you to know it's OKAY not to have all the answers.

2. It's OKAY to be "fearful." As young men, we don't like to be able to say, "I'm scared," because we were taught not to be scared. I'm telling you it's OKAY to be fearful, it's OKAY. Embrace that. Embrace the fact that you can acknowledge that you're fearful. You're human. Fear is NOT weakness. Fear is only temporary – it too shall pass.

3. It's OKAY to "trust." When mentors come into your life – LISTEN. Don't automatically think, "I'm not going to listen to him because he's not my mom or my dad," or "he doesn't know me and/or my story," etc. Sometimes God puts people in our lives who are meant to be there for a season or reason. That reason or season could be to help you become a better man. You have to be able to soak it up, you have to be able to say, "I got that, I needed it." Accept mentorship as a gift, and participate FULLY in it.

In conclusion, God has given each one of us certain gifts and talents that we must develop and use for the benefit of others (and ourselves). Along the journey of manhood, we will make plenty of mistakes and oftentimes experience doubt, confusion, and chaos. We have to realize that this journey is NOT a sprint. It is a marathon. It is a process that requires endurance and a commitment that must outlast any emotions. If you keep this as a principle–ANYTHING IS POSSIBLE.

BIO

L. L. Leonard is a native of Dallas, Texas, and has an extreme passion for serving people. He is commonly referred to as "L.L." Leonard by many of his colleagues and friends. His students and life coaching clients simply refer to him as "Coach" Leonard. He is a husband, father, teacher, volunteer, life coach and mentor. In all of those roles, he understands that his "LOVE for people" is his greatest gift. This is what fuels his capacity to serve in so many facets.

Coming from the inner-city Dallas, and being exposed, as well as enduring so many of the hardships common in urban America like poverty, high crime, violence, poor educational conditions, and fatherless homes, Mr. Leonard understands the responsibility to improve those conditions.

After being blessed with the opportunity to experience some successes in academics, athletics and entrepreneurship, Mr. Leonard decided to open barbershops and hair salons in various communities to serve people and create economic opportunities for others. This eventually manifested itself into a platform to serve people in different ways outside the scope of barbering/beauty. This was the birth of his journey as a public speaker, life coach and mentor.

www.LLLeonard.com

....

13

Recognize the Foundations of Success
By Kevin Anthony Johnson

When we think of our modern heroes in the arts and business world: Jay-Z, Earvin "Magic" Johnson, Russell Simmons, Daymond John or Kanye West easily come to mind because we see their success. They embody all of the material success that our culture applauds. We celebrate the story of their "overnight" prosperity and hope to emulate their swag. We tend to avoid looking beneath the surface to see the massive foundation that took years of planning, persistence, struggle, growth, resilience, failure, and self-reinvention to build.

Life happens to all of us – handing us bricks that we can choose to throw to the ground in frustration, or use to build our lives. All that I've been through, learned and applied, has made me into the man I am today. I am now a certified executive coach that has worked with leaders from over 18 different nations as part of an elite team of leadership coaches. I've built a life coaching practice over the past 18 years, helping business owners develop success mindsets and improve relationship skills. I now work for PricewaterhouseCoopers, the largest consulting firm in the world. I hold a Master's degree in transformational leadership, and I make a six-figure salary.

But if you simply evaluate me on those credentials, you'd miss that at age 19 I was homeless, carrying around my belongings in garbage bags, and living in friends' basements for nearly two years. You'd miss that I've been bankrupt twice, evicted from my childhood home, married and then divorced, lost my mother to lung disease, and started and closed businesses and nonprofit organizations. I used every credit card I had to build a production studio to follow my creative dreams just as the dot-com bubble burst, and I was reduced to bidding so low on a project to land the job that I didn't have enough money for a hotel and slept in my car for four nights in upper Michigan while doing a video shoot for the state.

We all make these kinds of choices every day whether we realize it or not.

I can remember feeling paralyzed by the difficulties I faced. It seemed like I could only see the negatives surrounding me and the impossibilities of the challenges I encountered. Not long after my family was evicted from my childhood home, I came across a book titled *Think and Grow Rich* by Napoleon Hill.

It was this book that awakened me to the power of my mind to change my circumstances and move out of victimhood. I shifted from seeing what couldn't be done – what I learned was scarcity-thinking – to noticing all of the possibilities around me, and what could be done – an abundance mindset. In this new abundant mindset, instead of being paralyzed, I made myself available to serve in whatever capacity I could find. I cleaned tables at the food court as an adult. I've painted rocks on suburban street curbs for 10 dollars. I've collected cans to gather a dollar to buy a bag of meat and a loaf of bread. I've cut hair to keep the lights on. I coached everyone who would let me work with them – hundreds of hours for free.

Here's the reason why this matters: The lessons I learned and the principles I now live by can be traced back to my choice to see possibilities instead of impossibility, to serve, and to focus on creating visible value for people. Each choice was a brick that was building me as a man. Each brick developed my sense of integrity and character. To be clear, I've made mistakes so embarrassing that I wanted to crawl under a rock – but the way I responded to those mistakes became a brick cemented in my character as well.

You can use your current situation as a stepping stone instead of a stumbling block when you choose to see the possibilities, choose to serve, and create visible value with your service.

These are things that no one can see when they look at me now, because if you see me now, you'll see the kind of house I live in and you'll see the kind of car I drive, but you won't see the bricks that it took for me to build to where I am right now. I moved to Chicago in 2005 with a small trailer, a failing marriage, a home in foreclosure, and bankruptcy pending. And in less than 10 years, I'd laid the bricks that built the foundation for me to now do work that makes a difference in the world AND provides me with a great lifestyle that I am deeply grateful for. This kind of transformation calls us to be able to harness all of our energies in service of something larger than ourselves.

Harness Your Masculine Power for the Highest Good

As you enter and move through young adulthood, you'll be faced with an ever-changing pulse between isolation as a man, and various levels of intimacy with others. By intimacy, I do not mean of the physical nature, but a sense of belonging in various groups. You may already feel these tugs to be a unique individual, but also to be part of a family or community that accepts you as you are. Making attempts to fill the voids of your life with sexual conquests and unhealthy relationships, can stifle your ability to fully live your dreams. This is an abuse (an abnormal use) of your masculine power.

As a man, you have a natural yearning to do, provide, protect, and give, while women tend to want to be, receive, create, and nurture. Men and women can share any of these qualities, but as a man, it's important to be purposeful about how you "do, provide, protect, and give."

My father was present in my home, but as an automotive executive and entrepreneur, I didn't get much time with him. As a result, I learned how to shave, how to talk with girls, and got my first sex advice from sources, like my equally ignorant teen friends and even the Encyclopedia Britannica (a printed version of Wikipedia from back in the day). I was clueless about the power of being a man – and reckless with that power.

Napoleon Hill wrote of a concept he called "sex transmutation," or the harnessing of our sexual energy for creative expression. Hill writes about how many of the captains of industry in his time (Carnegie, Rockefeller, etc. ...) channeled their sexual energy and their creative energy toward productive ends.

You've got boundless sexual energy in your youth and you can spend it on sexual conquest or building something that lasts. You can constructively use the resource of your sexual, creative energy to take action and generate ideas that are in alignment with your vision for your life.

The act of sex is a powerful one – but we can engage in sex where it requires nothing from us emotionally, spiritually, or intellectually. You're capable of being far more innovative and visionary by powerfully channeling and re-directing your masculine power. This is about you using the energy to create something that provides solutions, something that is prosperous, or something that could even changes lives, instead of just "knocking boots" with a woman. Yes, you can re-direct and use your sexual energy to manifest great things into reality in your life.

Bring your whole person, physical, spiritual, emotional and mental, into creating something that adds value to the world. My questions to you are: *What is the vision you want to build in the world? What's the legacy you want to leave behind?* The more you focus on what you truly desire out of life, the clearer your vision will become.

We Are Designed to Thrive Together

I decided that I want to inspire, equip and empower other people to live their dreams. I set out to be an excellent listener, expose myself to big ideas and big thinkers, ask and entertain big questions, and learn how to relate to many different types of people. This mindset of exposure and desiring to do and be more, contributes to my continuous learning and growth as a man, father, friend and global citizen.

Surround yourself with people who support you and those who challenge you to grow -we need both forces working on our behalf. It's vital to be who you are and to always be in the process of becoming more of yourself. The world needs you to be distinct – fully yourself – bringing the unique offering of yourself and all of your gifts and skills and talents. You are an essential brick in this building called humanity. The truth is, we need each other to thrive.

The fact that you are reading my words right now makes you a brick in my life. I see myself in you. We are made of the same clay. I was that young man searching for mentors, hungry for guidance in how to be a man and how to navigate this precious gift called life. Writing this to you has revealed things to me that I wouldn't have thought of if not for this project, which is designed to reach you.

My gift is now to be a positive part of your experience and perhaps, one day, you will harness your gift in such a way that it reaches back to touch other lives too. Science tells us that we are wired for connection. It is natural for us to desire to want to be in relationship with other people – our lives depend upon this. Remember, you don't have to go at it alone. There's no shame in asking for help. We're designed to thrive when we work together.

BIO

Kevin Anthony Johnson (Coach KJ) is an executive coach and entrepreneur who has worked with leaders and teams around the world on leadership and culture change. He has hosted important conversations from Shanghai to Chicago's South Side, and loves to mentor young leaders, dance, and make all kinds of art.

coachkj@gmail.com

14

Over Everything, Love
By W. Lenny Howard

"Love takes off masks that we fear we cannot live without and know we cannot live within." - James Baldwin, "The Fire Next Time," 1963

I am writing this because I want you, my young brother, to know I love you and you have greatness inside of you. Hopefully, you can benefit from my experiences and struggles. As men we do not often hear another man telling us that they love us, especially a stranger. As black males, we are taught to be strong, to be the providers, to endure at all costs, but we are not taught to love ourselves or others, to be vulnerable, or to be emotionally connected. It took me a long time to understand the importance of self-love, of accepting me and others for who we are — the good and the bad. We need this type of love in our lives to be able to forgive. Love and forgiveness are the foundations of a life worth living.

I am not the same person, a decade ago, that I am now. I was arrogant and overambitious, and mostly concerned with status, career, money and material things. I did not like this version of myself. I went to a small college and was fairly popular, which translated into a lavish amount of attention from the opposite sex. Perhaps it started in college when I was more "confident" and "self-assured" than during high school. And while my intentions were never to hurt anyone, all of my choices generated reactions and consequences — consequences for which I did not immediately accept responsibility.

That self-centered outlook on life was tested ten years ago as I stood in a church preparing to marry for the first time. Two things ran through my mind: one, this woman is a good person but we should not be getting married; and two, one of my best friends of 17 years, was not at my wedding.

As I stood at that altar, vowing to love another forever, I did not have a clear understanding of what it meant to be a man or how to love a wife. I did not understand who I was at the time. If I had known more clearly my authentic self, I would have made different decisions about my wedding and about pushing away a valuable friendship.

If you are anything like my younger self, and many young men are, then I want to share what I've learned. I developed a process over 26 years that has helped me discover my authentic self and the love that comes from self-acceptance and forgiveness. I have struggled with every stage in the process but along the way, someone else believed in me enough to ask me difficult questions, just as I believe in you:

Take Off Your Mask. Discover and Accept Your Authentic Self

Your life's journey is an exploration and celebration of you — all of your wonderful qualities and all of your faults. You must be prepared to answer difficult questions about who you are, and be willing to take off any "fake masks" to get to the place where your decisions aren't based only on needs and wants. This process is not about viewing things in terms of right and wrong, but rather, exploring what you like about yourself and what you want to improve upon. Years ago, when I began to remove my mask and truly look at myself, I had to think about and justify a series of poor decisions about past relationships. Thinking about those memories made me feel horrible all over again. It was like watching a movie of my life and they were only showing all the bad stuff.

Being honest means seeing yourself as you currently are, not being hyper-critical or overly focused on the bad aspects of your life more than the good ones, or vice versa. This is not about good or bad, it is about continuing to discover and uncover the things you like about yourself and making adjustments to the parts of yourself that you want to improve. This first step is challenging but necessary.

Impact. How are your choices impacting you and those around you?

Every day you make a series of choices — some are mindless like opening a door or brushing your teeth; others are more purposeful, like leaving a voicemail message or saying something hurtful about someone else so that others will laugh.

In isolation, these choices can seem harmless and unrelated, but when you look at them closer, they form a series of choices — a pattern. This pattern of choices is what makes up your life. You are the living product of all your choices.

During my senior year of high school, my physics teacher taught us Isaac Newton's third law of motion — for every action there is an equal and opposite reaction. Now that I've "grown up" some, I understand how that law shows up in my everyday life. Every day I make choices that impact someone other than myself. And every day, whether you are aware of it or not, you make choices that impact someone else other than yourself. It is important to be aware of how people are uplifted or hurt by your choices and actions.

In general, young men between the ages of 15 and 24 tend to be very self-centered. During that time in my life, I operated from that self-centered space and didn't take responsibility for the impact or effect of my words, choices and actions, nor did I realize how I emotionally impacted other people, especially women. Moreover, I didn't realize that our interactions made a long lasting impact on both of us.

Take a moment to think about the impact of your recent decisions on others. Now take it a step further and consider the consequences your decisions will have two years from now.

I share this because the process of understanding who you are and still loving that person after you answer them can be HARD! It can uncover some painful memories and hard-to-face truths about your character. However, this is not the time to quit. This is the time to persist, to lean in, and continue looking honestly at the reflection in the mirror without the mask. At that time when I looked in the mirror, I liked only *parts* of my reflection. Luckily, Newton's third law is occurring with *every* action and reaction, so you can begin now making better choices that yield different and *better* reactions.

Allow Love Into Your Life

Love made me want to be a better man! It made me want to think about someone else instead of only thinking about myself. My current wife, Keisha, and I met in college and reconnected again after my divorce. She has chosen to love me even though I have made many horrible choices in my past. She accepts all of me and I, all of her. It taught me love is about the combining of two people into one focus. The "me" becomes "we." I use this example to highlight that my focus has shifted from being self-centered to now being others-centered. In full disclosure, I am still a work in progress and I still have my selfish moments, but I take responsibility for them and continue to make better choices. These steps are not about being perfect, they are about, step by step, becoming a better man and better person.

With Love Should Come Forgiveness

Learning forgiveness is the final part of the process. Without it, emotions like resentment and anger can override all of your hard work. Forgiveness is a humbling experience because *it starts with forgiving yourself, first.*

One example is the best friend I mentioned in the beginning of this essay became my best friend during the summer after eighth grade and we remained best friends through high school, college, and into our late 20s. We were closer than friends —we were brothers.

I chose not to invite him to my first wedding because our friendship was in a transitional place, so at the time, we were not speaking. However I invited his parents to my wedding. I did understand the impact of that decision because I was focused on my needs and wants. His parents were my second mom and dad so I wanted them there on that day. *The consequences of excluding him at such an important life event ended our friendship.* I was so angry that I did not think about how he felt by not being invited or the awkward position I put his parents in by asking them to choose between me on this special day, or support him, by not attending the event.

My wife and I divorced three years later and I had to begin a process of finding *"myself"*. I share this because I had to re-learn how to love and forgive myself. I had to release that emotional pain and regret I was burdened with because I had lost my best friend and I now had a failed marriage.

My process of forgiveness involved journaling and a lot of conversations with God. I used a notebook to write down all of my thoughts and emotions. I needed to write because I had all these emotions and regrets swirling around in my head, keeping me up at night, and I did not know what else to do. Putting what was in my head down on paper helped me to make sense of everything..

I was stuck reliving that poor choice over and over again, and the only way out was forgiveness. I took the notebook with all my emotions and pain inside, said a prayer to God, and burned it outside in my barbeque grill.

Forgiveness allowed me to release negative emotions and have the freedom to make better decisions. I also promised that when I saw my friend again, I would be completely honest and tell him, "I'm sorry for not inviting you to my wedding. I am sorry for any strain it may have put on your relationship with your parents." Forgiveness is when you can think about an event from your past but you are no longer experiencing the emotions from the event.

I am very proud to report that when I finally saw him again, we spoke and I said exactly what I had promised. I confessed that during that period in my life, I was making a lot of poor and short-sighted choices. Not inviting him to my wedding but inviting his parents was a low blow and a decision I regretted. I let him know that I was sorry for making that choice. He agreed, and accepted my apology and request for forgiveness. It took a while to rebuild our friendship, and it's almost back to where it was in eighth grade. Our friendship got a second chance because of forgiveness. Love and forgiveness are the foundations of being a better man and having healthy relationships with others. I've learned to value love over everything.

Manhood is hard work. It takes sacrifice and is rooted in honesty and character. Being a man is about more than "providing" and taking care of others. You must also take care of yourself and learn to love yourself. The best way to take care of yourself is with love and forgiveness. With love in your heart guiding your decisions, you will make better ones. When you make a mistake, take responsibility for it. When you offend someone, give them a sincere apology. Forgiveness has the power to heal. It can restore a broken heart and restore a broken friendship. With love and forgiveness in your life and in your heart— you can change the world!

BIO

W. Lenny Howard currently works as an independent educational consultant. He earned his Bachelor's of Arts from Saint Mary's College of Maryland, his Master's in School Counseling from Loyola College of Maryland, and his Doctorate in Educational and Organizational Leadership from the University of Pennsylvania. He currently lives in Maryland with his loving wife Keisha, who does international communications work, and their beautiful son Koa.

w.lenny.howard@gmail.com

. . . .

15

Position, Purpose and Power:
A Lesson in Servant Leadership
By Darnell J. Head

My early years read much like the average urban black male tale. It begins with a clear beginning where things were normal by all appearances, followed by a sequence of events that led to a life-changing climax, which concluded with lessons learned.

Our experiences may be very similar. In fact, whatever your background, you may find that we have much in common. Perhaps you are going through a struggle that seems too great to overcome. You must understand that there will always be a victor at the end of the journey, and for you and me, a victorious outcome is our only option.

I recall being on a trip to Cincinnati as a fifth-grade student with my fellow middle school performing arts classmates. We were a traveling acting club scheduled to perform at the local university. As the only child of my three siblings given the opportunity to explore his talents in such a way, I never failed to recognize this privilege.

From this time, through eighth grade, I enjoyed my lifestyle as I took on the personality and fortune of my classmates, who unlike myself, were from stable homes. As one of the few black males in this school, I found myself experiencing the difference between being black or white and being rich or poor. I was not surprised or even unhappy of falling into the "poor black" category but I knew that I could not get comfortable in that state of mind; I wanted more for myself.

Reality set in when we moved from Akron, Ohio, to Detroit, Michigan, where I would live the next five years in a lifestyle that paled in comparison to the years which preceded it. If you are in a home where bills are rarely paid, food is scarce, and domestic violence is common, you can understand and relate to the home I experienced.

My family strived to be rich in character but we remained poor in every economic sense of the word. Not only did we lack the basic essentials, such as three meals a day, but my siblings and I witnessed multiple episodes of domestic violence between my parents that would often leave my mother physically and emotionally broken. Throughout my neighborhood and families close to mine, I saw black men regularly take part in drugs, violence, and abuse. This dysfunction only added to the confusion of what it meant for me to be a black male.

Emergence of a Black Male

I had always known I was a black male, but I was not aware that I was not the "customary" stereotype of the *hood* black. I was too proper, too cultured, too intelligent, too articulate, and too optimistic according to what my urban black male peers deemed acceptable. I far exceeded the very low "black bar" that my new community had set.

This low black bar left me feeling misunderstood and confused about what it meant to be a black male. I felt that as long as I was smart and talented with the hope of a future, I was somehow not falling into line with the prevailing low expectations for black males. Observing the black male examples on television, in popular music, in my community, and even my family, it seemed that I was not supposed to succeed and foolish of me to think otherwise. I felt that I had to remain just beneath the low black bar to remain relevant, popular, and in compliance with what society expected of me.

By the time I turned 15, my family was split. The volatile home to which we were all accustomed ended with my mother seeking haven in a shelter, and my father serving stints in the local jail. With both of my parents out of the home and essentially all lines of support suddenly gone, I was left to take on the responsibility of caregiver and provider for my two younger siblings.

This meant I enrolled us into schools – myself transferring high schools six times during this two-year period. I even moved us multiple times into homes where we would not pay rent, resulting in evictions. After each eviction, I would find us another home and another school to attend. There was no consistent adult figure present and we remained on our own. I gracefully took on the role of full-time high school student, and full-time employee. I worked 40 hours a week as a student. I went through life daily knowing that my siblings only ate when I brought cold food home from work.

Such instability led me to sell marijuana and anything else I could get my hands on. I used the money to purchase stolen cars and resell them on the streets. I had no driver's license, but I would drive myself and my siblings around the city, to and from school. I was arrested and jailed five times in two years for these offenses. Never once did a judge inquire about how I found myself in his courtroom. Had even just one judge asked me, he would have recognized the challenges I faced as the sole support of myself and my siblings. I began to understand that while I was a product of my environment and circumstance, the direction of my life was a direct reflection of how I decided to respond to my challenges.

From age 15-18 I inherited this great responsibility. I did not feel anger, sadness or frustration with this. Instead, I felt motivated and purposed. I could not understand why I did not have the happy, stable life many teens were fortunate to have, but I knew that my family depended on me. My drive to hold things together was far more necessary during this time than they had ever been.

Self-Determination

School guidance counselors are known for their support, leadership and development. They typically lead their students down a track which allows them to maximize their potential. The most transformative moment of this period in my adolescence occurred when the guidance counselor of my fifth high school, instead of encouraging me, instructed me to drop out midway through my senior year. My unstable home and extensive legal record had me labeled an early failure. Believing what the guidance counselor said about my potential and lack of stability, I heeded her word and did just as I was guided to do – I dropped out of school, four months shy of graduating.

The moment of transformation did not occur right away for me. I felt a false sense of liberation in her directive, not realizing just how dangerous that was. It took only a few weeks before I decided to act out against my circumstance and potential failure. I understood that for the last two years I had developed into a force that would not easily falter in the face of a challenge. I had been jailed, abused by officers, and neglected by the courts, and now my school system. In the same instance, I made myself a survivor, a catalyst, optimist and pioneer. Before long, I recognized that there was purpose in my journey.

I determined that ultimately it was up to me to capitalize on my purpose and maximize the opportunities presented to me. Although my circumstance and position in life had erected a series of barriers, I decided to take control of the few things that I could. I wanted to be a success in life and no one was going to stop me from accomplishing this.

Upon this reflection, I arose to push forth under my own will and determination. One month after dropping out, I enrolled back into high school. Despite being told that high school graduation was a non-possibility for my life, I defied expectations and saw myself through to graduation that same year, and even on to college.

Perhaps you have come to the point in your life now that you must access your level of self-determination to overcome the obstacles you face. What you must remember is that the ability and will to become more than the statistical criminal, school dropout, or poor black male, is naturally within you.

Purpose in Your Position

A point to draw from my trials and triumphs is that I learned to take charge in my position. We all have a position in life. Some of us are fathers, others are sons and brothers. In my position, I found myself playing the role of brother, caregiver, student, repeat offender and friend. This illustrates my physical position. It took time for me to understand *why* this was my position. It was not until I was able to reflect, and well into my professional career, that I came to recognize that everything I had gone through, each struggle, each conflict, each victory, was to align me to God's divine design for me life.

The first revelation in this reflection is best articulated by simply saying I had to first recognize that there was *purpose in my position*. I took what was being perceived as a life of failure and no possibility, and began to see it instead as a purposed position. While it was not clear to me why and how I had found myself in such a position, the basic instincts of service and leadership immediately kicked in. I now reframed my life circumstances so that I could see how I had been "forced" to lead a life of service from a young age. This "showed up" in the form of me taking responsibility for being of service to my siblings when my parents were both incapacitated. My service was also evident by working late hours each night while still going to school. The decision to complete high school instead of giving up was in service to what would best position me to support my family. Great leaders would call this Servant Leadership.

Servant leaders understand the circumstances of those that depend on them for guidance and support. The servant leader is a servant first. Servant leadership arises from the natural desire to want to serve others. With this mind-set, servant leaders approach challenges as a service to some higher need. For me, I was made to lead in service of the needs and well-being of my family, and I approached these difficulties as an opportunity to serve.

As a servant leader I acted then as I do now: with the intent and purpose to lead through service. What this required was an act of selflessness that formulated the foundation of my leadership and success. My saving grace was and will remain the willingness to think of others first. In service to my siblings, I was able to think less of my own personal needs, and focus on their success and progress. And in this, there remained purpose in my position.

Consider where you are right now. Evaluate your life. Take in your surroundings and begin to develop an understanding of your position. The troubles you face, whether small or large, are not by chance. Each event, circumstance, or situation you encounter has the ability to build within you the strength of character that will increase your ability and availability to lead. I found my rightful position, to lead through servitude, during my most troubled years. *How is your position strengthening your leadership?*

Power in Your Position

I have never questioned my position, and I encourage you to embrace and not question yours. I was exactly where I should have been and when I needed to be there. I was positioned to serve and to lead, while seeing to the progress and development of myself and my family. I used foresight to focus on where I was headed while also remaining aware of my position. In this, I was enabled to accept the *power* in my position. In your position, whatever that may be, you have the power to change lives, yours being the first.

You may think that your position is too difficult for you to have any true power. Great struggles are only entrusted to those who can handle the journey and live to sing the victories of the trek. There is a definite *power* in that. The *power* for me was revealed in my continued leadership beyond college; obtaining master's and doctorate degrees, becoming an educator and a pioneer of cultural awareness, and witnessing my siblings become leaders themselves. That was the power in my position then, as it is now.

The challenge before you is to first identify your position, and secondly, the purpose in your position. This supports you in better understanding and fully embracing the *power* in your position. I, and many others like me, overcame because we simply would not accept the alternative, which would have undoubtedly led us down a path of self-destruction, imprisonment, and failure. This is not a decision that YOU can arrive at without understanding the sheer power YOU naturally hold.

You are gifted and have within you everything you will ever need to succeed and become the master of your fate. I challenge you to maintain the habit of thinking positive thoughts and taking the positive actions that will allow you to identify the purpose of your position, while maximizing the power in your position. Take "ownership" of your position and you will prevail! You are powerful, you are capable, and you are destined for greatness.

BIO

Darnell J. Head received a Bachelor of Science in Criminal Justice from Grand Valley State University, and a Master's of Education and Doctorate of Education from Concordia University. During his college experience, Darnell led various organizations and community initiatives to address a very racially insensitive climate. Darnell later became an elementary school teacher, educating students in Los Angeles, Grand Rapids, Michigan, and Chicago. Darnell has also worked with students abroad in various countries of Central America. Since 2008 he has partnered with cultural organizations to promote cultural inclusion and understanding on college campuses, while also working closely in partnership with education reform organizations. Darnell currently leads Cultural Competence LLC., providing cultural consultation to institutions and organizations across the nation.

darnellhead@cultureshockent.com

. . . .

16

Purposeful Manhood
By H. James Williams

"Purposeful Manhood means developing into manhood to fulfill a useful purpose in life."

How does a boy or young man come to know about the essence of manhood for his success in life? Who are the individuals he can trust with his vulnerability and uncertainty of what is best for him? What meanings of courage and spiritually should he adopt to purposefully honor becoming a man? By whose definition should he become a man?

During my formative years, my sense of *Purposeful Manhood* was ambiguous at best. I witnessed my father work and hustle hard to provide for his family. At home, he was quick to punish childhood misbehavior. His life became my earliest perceptions of manhood. Upon turning 17 years old, I made the choice to leave home rather than abide by a 9 p.m. curfew established by my father. I worked part time and managed to barely finish high school.

It is important for us to acquire skills to provide for ourselves, to know how to manage our money, and to surround ourselves with people we can trust to give us the best advice possible in life. Acquiring the best education possible will help you make good decisions for your life. In the years after I left home, many individuals imparted wisdom into me about becoming a man and I would like to share a few of those nuggets of wisdom with you.

Work, Family and Determination

My late parents Carrie and Howlett Williams, both with limited education and means, taught me that an able-bodied man who would not work when given the opportunity to earn an honest wage, was not deserving of food and shelter. They taught me that life would not always be easy, and that my personal determination would be necessary to survive the toughest situations. Even though I left home at an early age, they planted the seed of thought within me that whatever you do, do it to the best of your ability with lots of integrity. I know now that love and determination sustained our family bond.

When you encounter difficulties in life and feel you have nowhere to turn, hopefully your family will be there to assist you. The love of family, or even having someone to look up to in the absence of family, is important to building your self-esteem and establishing your sense of confidence.

My high school assistant principal, the late Donald Howard, counseled me to have focus in life and to wholeheartedly commit to learning and self-improvement. He sought out to instill me with self-confidence, and believed in me over any doubts I had about myself. He taught me to have self-determination, to value personal excellence, and to never allow another to take my self-worth away from me. His words still challenge me whenever I have doubts about myself. Find someone, or allow someone, like him into your life.

Learning and Respect

The late Ben M. Becker, my high school principal, gave me a ride home from school one day and talked to me about the value of studying, passion, and having respect for others. Education was his passion and his first love. He emphasized that learning with passion can improve your outlook on life. Your passion for learning comes easier when you know the field of study that excites you, and you choose to pursue it. He taught me that respect is earned, and you have to work at any endeavor to show your competence. I have learned that to be really good at whatever you pursue in life, you should choose the path that is heart-centered. Your calling in life is attached to what's in your heart.

Mr. Becker also coached freshman boxing, and for more than 60 years he worked with the U.S. Olympic program in a number of distinguished positions, including boxing commissions, committees and sports teams. He coached Muhammad Ali (Cassius Clay) to his 1960 gold medal in the light-heavyweight division and helped develop the career of Sugar Ray Robinson.

One day during my senior year in high school, I recall him having another male student and me put on boxing gloves in the school basement to settle our differences rather than engage in an after-school fight. Each of us, after getting in a few good punches, took off the gloves after reeling from each other's punches. We talked through our differences, cemented our friendship and departed the school grounds with mutual respect for each other. We never had a physical altercation again. More than anything, this encounter taught me to avoid situations where outside individuals instigate and provoke hatred and violence for their amusement and personal agendas.

Romance, the Opposite Sex and Children

My first full-time job upon honorable discharge from the United States Army, and refusing unemployment compensation, was as a hospital janitor. Although I was not fully prepared financially and intellectually to be a dad when my children were born, I labored in love as best I knew how in order to give them a better life. Their mother and I, regardless of any personal differences, always put the best interests of our children first.

Most of us, as young men have been told to avoid getting a girl pregnant, as if that is all there is to know about women. But the most clarity I came to have about women, in my opinion, is that they are the closest things on earth to angels. Women are very special creations by which the Creator manifests His purpose within this world. Every human that has ever walked this earth was born through the body of a woman.

What person, as a child, has never cried out, *"Mommy"* or *"Mama"* in moments of distress before learning to exclaim, *"God help me!"*? I view mothers as God's emissaries. True manhood honors, values and respects the qualities of intellect, wholesomeness, and creative ingenuity in a woman. Fathering a child is not evidence of responsible fatherhood nor is giving birth to a child evidence of responsible motherhood. Parenthood is a two-person endeavor involving mutual respect.

Here are more things I have learned along the way that have made me understand what purposeful leadership really means...

Leadership and Service

Mentors in my life generally taught me about leadership. I learned being a leader meant rendering service to those the leader is entrusted to lead. Good leadership is about being of service to others, and is never about personal, or selfish gain. Leadership involves showing the courage to forge ahead in the face of fear and adversity when the outcomes of your decisions and actions affect more than you. Leadership is about not letting past negative consequences stand in the way of hope and righteousness for the future. It is with this sense of leadership that I served in executive management positions in federal and state government and as an educator and community mediator.

Being of Service to Your Community

Community service of any kind that improves lives on any scale is a service of great personal reward and satisfaction to your soul. We want to be sure to be a blessing to others and not a burden. It would be wise to volunteer, where possible – within communities locally and globally – to strengthen your leadership skills. I still volunteer in my community, with the hope of making a difference in the lives of others. I've found that my service allows me to "pay it forward" and help others after all of the help and support I've received from others in my life.

Your days on earth are numbered. As a man, you want to be able to look back over your life and be able to determine what positive purpose your life served, what your usefulness was, how you spent your days, what your legacy is, and what difference you made in the lives of others and in the world. My hope is that at the end of my manhood journey, my presence on earth will have made a lasting and positive difference in someone's life.

BIO

Williams owns and operates Aliant Coaching Services in Baltimore, Maryland. He is a certified personal coach and publishes inspirational booklets and posters. He is the author of several books, two of which are titled, "*Wavelets of Purpose*" and "*Addae's Journey*".

hwilliams@aliantsecuritygroup.org

. . . .

17

Decisions

By Thomas Cotton, MAUM

The Challenge

One of the biggest issues I had growing up was the absence of my father. Most young men at one time or another have at least had an opportunity to meet their fathers, even if their father was not active in their lives. However, I never had the opportunity to meet mine, even to this day.

I have never been one to blame other people for the failures in my life, but if my father would have chosen to be an active part of my life, I do believe some things would have been a little bit different. Due to this, I indirectly experienced my first major form of rejection, and at the time I didn't even know it. This feeling of what felt like rejection would later cause me to begin to make very poor decisions. Though I had an incredible mother and grandmother, they were only able to do so much. I was also an only child and that was a challenge for me because I had no siblings to protect me. Being an only child made the temptation to fit in really big for me at the same time.

As an outlet for my emotional baggage, I began to smoke marijuana, drink alcohol, become sexually active, and then finally I became affiliated with the neighborhood gang, "The Black Stone Nation." To make matters worse, I attended Calumet High School, which was one of the worst high schools that you could attend on the South Side of Chicago. Calumet had more of a reputation for gang violence and high school dropouts than it did for their academics and graduates.

During my time there, I did not go to class. My freshman and sophomore years were a struggle due to fighting, because at that time, there were more members of the opposite gang. I recall one day as school was being dismissed and we were leaving the building, we heard gunshots. When we ran to the exit door, we found my friend laid out on the ground outside covered in blood, shot once in the back.

At the time, I didn't realize how blessed I was to come from a home with stability. Instead of being a person that influenced others to do the right thing, I became highly influenced by people who were doing the wrong things. In my neighborhood, if you did not do what everyone else was doing (gang banging), you were considered to be an outcast. And in some cases, you were even treated like the opposition.

*I know the challenges you might be facing, but you do **not** have to be a victim of your circumstances, surroundings or upbringing. You must use the challenge to gain clarity on what you want. Find someone you admire and respect, whether in your school, church, or in your neighborhood, and ask them for guidance so that you don't make the same mistakes and avoid some huge pitfalls.*

Christian Values

Growing up in a home with a Christian mother and grandmother was also a challenge within itself because I learned right from wrong. Although I talked about being gang-affiliated, smoking weed and drinking, there was still the Christian values they instilled in me that knew the things that I was doing were not right.

Going to church played a major part in my life as well. The church was the place, besides within my home, where I learned solid values. On the other hand, because there wasn't a specific group created for youth at my church, such as a Youth Ministry, I was still left to the negative influencing ideologies of my neighborhood.

Although I never really had a male influence in my life, there was one gentleman by the name of Ron Crenshaw who did the best he could to try and teach us to make better decisions. Ron was our neighborhood gym instructor who actually cared about the well-being of each and every one of us. But because his positive view of life was not popular among us, we rebelled against his advice and insight. If many of us had listened to him, some of our lives could have changed direction for the better.

In 1991, my senior year, I was expelled from Calumet High School and required to attend an alternative high school by the name of Olive Harvey Middle College. This opportunity became a blessing for me that had an immediate impact in my life from day one.

I remember sitting in orientation on day one, waiting to stand and introduce myself as was the custom for new students. I noticed something very different about this environment – there wasn't any loud talking, the current students were respectful to the teachers, and when Mrs. Helen Hawkins, the principal, would attempt to get a student's attention, she would address him or her as "scholar." This was very strange for me. To top it off, once I stood up and introduced myself, Mrs. Hawkins looked at me and said, "Your name is Terrific Thomas." I knew she viewed my transcript, and knew why I had been expelled, but what I realized later is that *she was not focused on who I had been – she was more focused on who I could become.*

If you ever feel like things will never change, remember: There is always hope. Your current situation can change for the better.

A Chance to Change

Attending Olive Harvey Middle College was one of the best things that could have happened to me at that time in my life. This would be the first time that I would go to school with individuals from different gangs, and most of us would get along. This would also be the first time that I would see, firsthand, what it looked like for teachers to actually care about the students. This would be the first time in my life where the thought of going to college would start to become a reality.

During my time there I would accomplish so much to only have been enrolled for one year. I became active in the student government, I graduated with honors, I was accepted into several colleges; I was looked at as a leader amongst my peers, and I graduated with the class notable of "Teacher's Pet" because of the relationship that I developed with the principal of the school. I missed only one day at Olive Harvey Middle College compared to the 100 plus days of cuts and multiple absences that I racked up at Calumet High.

While there, I began to recognize that there was a difference between myself and the average youth in my neighborhood. It was not that I was better than any of them, but I was beginning to realize that a positive seed was now planted in my life. I began to realize that I was at a crossroad, and I needed to decide if I was going to move toward positive change or if I would stay in what appeared to be a normal but highly toxic community.

God had given me a chance for change, a chance to be different and a chance to make a difference, although I had initially allowed my environment and circumstances to define who I was. The seed that was ultimately awakened in me was a seed of greatness; *a seed that was already within me,* and a seed that informed me that I did not have to settle any longer.

*I know life can be hard and seem unfair, but you must be willing to stare your life in the face and tell Life that you will **not** back down, you will **not** settle, and you will **not** allow negative people to determine your destiny or dictate to you what your life should ultimately be. But you have to continue to press on.*

Sometimes Change Takes Time

Looking back now, I noticed how it was almost a 12-year journey to change completely after high school. Once again, I can see how those seemingly small decisions earlier in my life dictated me making more serious and detrimental decisions later. I ended up paying steep consequences later in my life – I got into some legal trouble. I was left in a situation where no one would hire me because I was a felon. I lost everything. I knew I had to do something. Something in me said, "Go back to school." It was not easy going back to school as an adult. Then I got married, so going to school as an adult and married was not easy. Then came the kids. It was tough because I still had to fight with those limiting thoughts. I had to fight through all the "You cant," and the "You'll never."

Be patient. It takes time to change complete, but if you stay committed, you can avoid making decisions that can negatively affect you later in life.

The Power of Making the Right Decisions

In the process of making decisions, you must first ask yourself:

What is the projected outcome of this decision? In other words, how will the decision you make today affect your life tomorrow? You must ask yourself: is it even worth you making this decision? There are some decisions that you will be confronted with that is not even worth your time (gang affiliation, bullying, drugs, sex, and not going to school). Finally, get someone who has more wisdom than you to walk alongside you in the decision-making process (parent, teacher, family member, or mentor).

It is imperative that you become an expert in making decisions because there are some things that cannot be avoided and you will be faced with the choices you made every day of your life. This does not mean you will be perfect in this process, but what it does mean is that your chances of making good solid decisions will increase.

Today I currently work in the same community where I grew up as a human service caseworker for the Illinois Department of Human Services. Every day, I see young men come into my office to apply for government assistance. Way too many of them have no education, can't get a job due to their criminal record, and some of them are even illiterate.

Often, I get a chance to speak one-on-one with them and almost every one of them says the same thing: "I wish I could do it all again."

Remember, you actually have the God-given responsibility and ability to choose a better life for yourself by making better decisions.

BIO

Thomas Cotton has over 10 years in ministry leadership. He holds a Bachelor's of Arts from Trinity International University with a concentration in Nonprofit Administration, Pastoral Leadership and Christian Counseling. He also holds a Master of Arts in Urban Ministry and Theological Studies. He currently serves as a Minister of the Gospel at New Life Celebration Church of God, where he also helps youth as a Youth Leader and has recently been appointed to the director of the New Life Institute School of Ministry.

While serving his community and working as human service caseworker for the state of Illinois, Thomas has discovered that there is a pressing need to help people discover the greatness that every individual possesses. Through the training he received upon joining the John Maxwell team, Thomas has recently launched "The Iron Factory." This service focuses on assisting people to remove the various obstacles that are preventing them from living their best life possible.

www.JohnMaxwellGroup.com/ThomasCotton